Deception

THE ART OF LIVING SERIES
Series Editor: Mark Vernon

From Plato to Bertrand Russell philosophers have engaged wide audiences on matters of life and death. *The Art of Living* series aims to open up philosophy's riches to a wider public once again. Taking its lead from the concerns of the ancient Greek philosophers, the series asks the question "How should we live?". Authors draw on their own personal reflections to write philosophy that seeks to enrich, stimulate and challenge the reader's thoughts about their own life. In a world where people are searching for new insights and sources of meaning, *The Art of Living* series showcases the value of philosophy and reveals it as a great untapped resource for our age.

Published
Clothes   *John Harvey*
Deception   *Ziyad Marar*
Fame   *Mark Rowlands*
Hunger   *Raymond Tallis*
Illness   *Havi Carel*
Pets   *Erica Fudge*
Sport   *Colin McGinn*
Wellbeing   *Mark Vernon*
Work   *Lars Svendsen*

Forthcoming
Death   *Todd May*
Middle Age   *Chris Hamilton*
Sex   *Seiriol Morgan*

Deception

Ziyad Marar

ACUMEN

For Tejeshwar

First published in 2008 by Acumen

Acumen Publishing Limited
Stocksfield Hall
Stocksfield
NE43 7TN
www.acumenpublishing.co.uk

ISBN: 978-1-84465-151-1

British Library Cataloguing-in-Publication Data
A catalogue record for this book is available
from the British Library.

Designed and typeset by Kate Williams, Swansea.
Printed and bound by Biddles Ltd, King's Lynn.

Contents

Acknowledgements

This book has changed and developed in many ways over the past few years. I would like to thank the people whose conversation, interest and support have been such a valuable backdrop to the writing process: in particular Kate Buchanan, Daniel Crewe, Jon Dickins, Geoff Lattimer, Dirk Snelders and my father Nael Marar, each of whom read and commented on some or all of the manuscript. I am also grateful to two anonymous reviewers for their constructive feedback.

Will Francis, my agent, has been enthusiastically engaged with my work from the beginning. His intelligent advice and consistent encouragement have been a key support throughout the process. I'm grateful to Mark Vernon, an exemplary series editor, for his detailed reading and comments, and would like to thank Steven Gerrard at Acumen for his critical eye and generous support of the project as well as Kate Williams for her unobtrusively skilful copy-editing.

I'm hugely grateful to my family whose patience I've tested severely over many a weekend and holiday in getting the book written. Kate, Anna, Ellie and Charlotte have provided a loving blend of cajoling and cheering that has sustained me throughout.

Finally, I would like to thank Tejeshwar (aka Bunny) Singh. His friendship and conversation over many, many years have enriched this project, and much else besides, in more ways than I can describe. My few days in his beloved "Valley View", in Landour in October 2007, were when I finished much of the script and it was the last time we were together before his untimely death. This book is dedicated to his memory.

... there is always some advantage in making men love us. Human life is thus only a perpetual illusion; men deceive and flatter each other. No one speaks of us in our presence as he does of us in our absence. Human society is founded on mutual deceit; few friendships would endure if each knew what his friend said of him in his absence ... (Pascal, *Pensées*)

Introduction

You may recall the poignant fable of the frog and the scorpion. The scorpion arrived at a stream he needed to cross and, since he couldn't swim, asked a frog nearby if she would take him across on her back. The frog, understandably sceptical, said, "No thanks, you'll just sting me." But the scorpion replied in a sweetly reasonable tone, "Why on earth would I sting you? I can't swim. If you die, I die." This made sense to the frog so she agreed to carry the scorpion to the other side. But as she was halfway across the stream she felt a violent stabbing pain in her side. She realized she had been fatally stung. As the frog began to sink under the water, dragging the scorpion to certain death, she asked, "Why did you sting me? Now you will die too." The scorpion replied, "It's in my nature."

This story contains many of the themes of this book. The conversation between scorpion and frog illustrates the way we struggle over deception and accountability. Was the scorpion's persuasiveness based on an outright lie or did he manage to deceive himself before deceiving the frog? Why did she believe him? Was it because of the logic of his argument or did his persuasive tone of voice make him sound sincere? If she had survived the sting would she have admitted her foolishness (caught out by a sham display of sincerity) or would she have found a way to rationalize her choice in retrospect (saying that anyone would have done the same)? And how do we explain the sting in the tail? Did the scorpion even *try* to resist the temptation? What did he really want? Did he in fact make a choice, or was the conclusion, as he suggests, predetermined and out of his hands. Can we hold the scorpion morally responsible for killing the frog? Can the scorpion be expected to answer the question "Why did I do that?" in any way reliably? Are we able to get to the truth of the matter or are we stuck with competing versions of what happened? Deception, whether of ourselves or of each other, runs through the texture of our lives.

In an obvious sense the opportunity for deception is greater today than ever before. In a highly mediated culture the proliferation of email, mobile phones and web communities ensures that many of our exchanges happen indirectly, leaving us unable to see the whites of each other's eyes. Meanwhile modern "enhancements", from Viagra to plastic surgery, help us cover up our weaknesses. Ours can seem like the age of propaganda. Service cultures wrap us in a soft tissue of insincerity ("Thank you for holding, your call is very important to us"), consumer cultures dole out endless promissory notes ("Where do you want to go today?") and telegenic politicians are more skilled than ever at spin. One way or another, the Western culture of impression management has effaced the distinction between perception and reality to a profound degree.

But to focus on these recent societal factors is to miss out on how the struggle to navigate between contradictions has always been fundamental to being human. As Immanuel Kant observed "Out of the crooked timber of humanity no straight thing can ever be made". And so we contrive to get our stories sounding straighter than we are. Sellers and buyers, parents and children, politicians and their electorate, employers and employees, friends, neighbours, colleagues and lovers all have reasons to deceive each other. The awkward fact is that your beliefs and mine do not converge that much. The same goes for what we desire.

Moreover we are also riven by *internal* conflicts. Cognitive dissonance is the background music to our daily hypocrisies as we bury our inconveniently mixed motives. Yet far from seeing consistency as "the hobgoblin of little minds", as Emerson advised, we crave it, along with acceptability and reasonableness; in short, we need credibility. In order to preserve our reputations we have to distort what we want and think so as to ignore the tensions. We flatter ourselves and each other, we exaggerate, bluff, falsify, conceal, dissemble, hoodwink, over-simplify, bury our heads and avert our gaze with such skill and speed that even we barely notice.

Deceptions bring consolations in tow. They help us to avoid many of the pains that an unvarnished account can yield, leaving us looking more competent and benevolent than we are. In fact the deceptions I explore in the following chapters are only occasionally deliberate or malign. This is not a book about how con artists swindle a life's savings from trusting pensioners, or, if it is, only tangentially. The deceptions I want to look at are central to the possibility of functioning as human beings who must deny the complexity of the world, and the contradictory nature of our beliefs and desires, if they are to get by. A proneness to falling for distorting illusions, an anxiety about being cheated, a willingness to give a good impression, the need to manage self-contradictory desires, to take unjustified credit and to duck the blame for regrettable choices all ensure that deception is intrinsic to being human.

But in order to deceive convincingly and with minimal guilt and anxiety it is helpful to delude ourselves first. Contrary to Descartes's use of the clear and distinct ideas that can come from true introspection, one of the more surprising insights from recent scholarship is a reconsideration of the unconscious. We deceive, but also deceive ourselves and each other about that very fact; that is, into believing that we are sincere. This second-level deception makes the mechanism so foolproof that it is intrinsically hard to detect. We can never hope to know ourselves well enough because there are large areas of our minds we have evolved not to know.

I want to explore this rich terrain in order to get a better understanding of how we might resist these tendencies. To be less deceptive and less prone to being deceived is to be more tolerant of our turbulence: whether our complexity, or how we change, or the awkward weight of our choices or the intimacies of conflict. It is to know that while our deceptions and consolations offer comfort, the price of this comfort is high, and there are benefits that come from resisting their lure as much as we can bear. On the other hand we need to come to terms with the fact that deception is an unavoidable part of living. Along the way I shall draw on philosophy, psychology and literature to explore the need to tell stories that place a good reputation above many other considerations. Using insights from literature and contemporary culture as well as scholarly work will, I hope, enrich the picture I want to paint; a picture that, despite inspiring ideals of authenticity and integrity, commits us to an irreducibly deceptive self-image, while offering a way to live well in this humbling light.

Later chapters will address many of these themes in turn. Chapter 2 looks at the contradictions of self-deception and weak will: how we con ourselves to help manage our mixed motives and wayward desires. Chapter 3 explores the vagaries of telling the truth to each other: the ways we deceive so as to maintain a good reputation and avoid the sting of shame. Chapter 4 reviews the moral choices we make and how good we are at scorpion-like self-exculpation, while exploring the constraints (both internal and external) on our capacity to choose well. And Chapter 5 concludes by assessing just how far we can get in challenging the comforting illusions that help us make sense of ourselves and each other.

The opening chapter sets the stage by looking at human nature and by arguing that, unlike real scorpions, humans evolved to tell stories that explain the world and each other in ways that are meaningful and persuasive. This process is underpinned by rapid unconscious processing that lies outside awareness, while shaping behaviour profoundly. The need to explain and believe runs so deep that people will grasp at straws to create fragments of meaningful order out of explanatory chaos. In the process we distort the evidence of our eyes and ears to interpret events in the world, as well as our own and others actions, and if we can't get the facts to fit we make things up.

1. *Homo credens*: the believer

In his book *Actual Minds, Possible Worlds*, the psychologist Jerome Bruner tells the story of a colleague who did a simple but interesting study. He took a list of twelve standard personality traits with positive and negative poles (such as lazy and energetic, honest and dishonest) and threw them together into random combinations of negatives and positives on a series of cards. He presented each card to a subject and asked them for a general description of the person depicted by those traits. Surprisingly the task was completed easily, every time, no matter how unlikely the combinations. No one ever said "It can't be done, there's no such person". Not once did these random combinations of characteristics elicit bafflement or hesitation on the part of the subjects. Bruner concluded (in the gendered language of his time) that with this "staggering gift for creating hypotheses … Man … is infinitely capable of belief. Surprising that he has not been described as *Homo Credens*" (1986: 51).

If we are infinitely capable of belief it is little surprise to see a correlative human vulnerability to deception and self-deception. If you lock too readily on to a way of seeing, a good description or a satisfying explanation you can easily be fooled. And we fool ourselves equally easily. According to recent research we assume we are quite a lot smarter, better looking and nicer than others think we are (and that's without alcohol). Only the depressed have a realistic self-image (note *realistic*, not pessimistic). People see conspiracy in cock-ups, tell and swallow tall stories (from fairy tales to films), and conjure up a hundred kinds of god with alacrity. In many cases, and contrary to logic, believing does actually make it so. The placebo effect, for instance, depends not on any active ingredient in the medicine but on nothing more than a *belief* in its efficacy. One might say the coin of social exchange among humans is *cred* in its different forms, stemming from the Latin *credere*, to believe or entrust. We are buffeted daily by its implications: if I am to give you credit, I need to find you credible, while avoiding the risk of seeming credulous in giving credence to your discreditable account. From religious *credos* to street cred, from professional credentials to political credibility, we trade in a currency that differs from that of all other animals. In trying to make plausible sense of the world and each other, unlike *actual* frogs and scorpions, we struggle over belief: what to believe, who to believe and how to seem believable. *Homo sapiens*, it seems, as Bruner said, is better named *Homo credens*: the believer.

It was Kant who observed that the world we inhabit and perceive depends on qualities of the perceiver's mind. Contrary to the previously widespread view of humans as passive containers of innate ideas, or recipients of pure experience, his "Copernican revolution" was to see us as trapped in a veil of appearances: a system of concepts and experience that constrain our perception of the world, and colour it profoundly. Metaphysical speculation about what lies beyond this world of appearances is incoherent, because it is a condition of having any experience at all that we impose certain features on it. These include the idea of cause and effect, the perception of events as ordered in time and objects as ordered in space.

In many ways Kant can be seen as a prescient and insightful psychologist. Steven Pinker's book the *The Stuff of Thought* attempts to cash out these fundamental Kantian concepts by showing how they are reflected in the building blocks of human languages. Language he says, gives us a clue about an *intuitive* physics that construes the world in terms of human purposes and goals rather than the non-teleological laws of nature. We make sense of the world in human terms, rather than explaining it in its own terms.

This view of language illuminates the fundamental mental models we use to make sense of our lives. Human languages contain: a concept of *space* embedded in prepositions, framed in terms of places and objects in qualitative relationship with each other; a conception of *time* embedded in tenses, framed as processes and events located on a single dimension; a conception of *matter* embedded in nouns (masses of stuff versus countable things stretched along one, two or three dimensions); and a concept of *causality* embedded in verbs (an actor directly impinging on an entity, knowingly, deliberately). Put these together and we build a picture of human rather than real physics that tells us about:

- the causal texture of the environment, that is, how we understand cause and effect;
- what is knowable, factual and willable;
- ways of packaging and measuring our experience;
- ways of assigning moral responsibility for events.

Human nature is configured to make sense of the world in a particular way, one that construes reality in terms that allow us to *reason* and *agree* about those aspects of reality that are *relevant* to our *purposes*. Our most basic perceptions of the world are thus profoundly constrained by certain ways of seeing. Similarly, as many empirical results demonstrate, at higher levels of thinking such as in reasoning and social interaction we see yet more deceptive patterns in the way we understand the world and each other. The point of this chapter is to explore aspects of human nature, quirks of human psychology, that lead us towards useful explanations of physical and social phenomena but also to deception, delusion and distortion.

The paths to belief are *crooked* in two senses: first they are not very logical, (following the biases, heuristics and good guesses that reflect the evolved texture of human thought), and second they depend for their consolatory power on self-deception. As we shall see, our proneness to illusions compels us to cook the facts quickly and effortlessly without knowing we have done so. The benefits of such explanations are clear enough – offering predictability, control, exculpation, simplicity and the reduction of conflict – and help us to dream up convincing explanations that make us seem coherent, consistent and blameless. But they come at a price, because the way we explain ourselves and each other is inevitably riddled with distortion and illusion. The first three sections of this chapter explore our proneness to illusion, whether perceptual, cognitive or narrative: how we diverge from the objective truth in conjuring up meaningful ways of explaining the world. The remaining sections address how we have evolved an array of unconscious skills both to spot cheats and to be persuasive to others. These skills, habits and the overreaching to which they make us prone set the foundation for the rest of the book.

Perceptual illusions

It is a universal feature of human brains that they carve up in a highly structured way what William James called the "blooming, buzzing, confusion" of sense data (1981: 462). They take rapid shortcuts; fill in gaps based on hypotheses about the world that evolved to help us survive in environments with high stakes and limited information. Let's start with how we literally "see" the world. One of the most remarkable things about our visual system is just how much we contribute unconsciously to what we see. It feels as if representations of the world pour, unaided, into our minds through our eyes, as through a window. Yet researchers have shown that vision is an active process that inventively *creates* much of what we see, turning the impoverished two-dimensional information on our retinas into a three-dimensional representation with many of the gaps filled in.

The "blind spot", a term so commonly enlisted to describe the limits of our attention in many contexts, sits quite literally in the back of the eye, at the head of the optic nerve where there are no photo-receptors. There ought to be a big blank in the middle of the visual field of each eye, but thanks to a feat of unconscious improvisation it is always filled in.

Look around and the impression you will have is of a smooth panorama, despite the fact that your visual world is actually a gappy one of brief and disjointed snapshots. The human gaze settles for a quarter of a second before jumping to the next scene. These *saccades* are quite rapid, usually lasting about 20 milliseconds or so, before the next pause. The reason we have difficulty sensing these rapid eye movements is that we are effectively blind during them. Our brains automatically fill in what we do not see, with what researchers delightfully term a "confabulation across saccades", to give us the experience of a continuous and stable scan.

Our visual perception seems effortless to us and it is only with cleverly designed optical illusions that we can get a glimpse of our own virtuosity. We can see this in the familiar Müller-Lyer illusion:

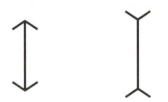

It is hard to see the vertical lines as of equal length, although they are. This is a consequence of the cues we normally rely on to gauge depth in the field of view. While the lines in the image above are the same length and so create the same length of representa-tion on the retina, our brains are fooled into making an adjustment because of the clues provided by the arrows. As you can see in the image below, it is a useful rule of thumb to see that arrows pointing inwards convey that the edge is oriented towards the viewer while the arrows pointing out imply the opposite. The innovative brain will "guess" that since they look the same length the one further away must be a longer line (since things loom large up close and shrink in the distance), which is how we end up perceiving it.

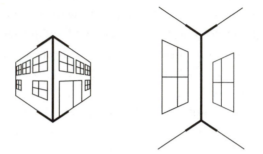

Another example is the Kanisza triangle:

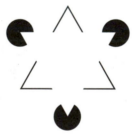

The missing wedges of the discs are like the points of a triangle so the brain fills in the gaps and "sees" a triangle that isn't really there, just to make sense of the diagram. This is relevant to my theme in a quite literal sense: we are prone to concocting illusions that anchor us in a way of seeing, very tightly, and these processes are to a large extent outside our control. In addition, the illusions persist *despite our second-order knowledge* that that is what they are. Even when I know the lines are the same length, or that there is no triangle, the illusion persists.

In her book *On Not Being Able to Paint*, Marion Milner found that she could not draw lines randomly – her "free drawings" kept veering into the recognizable far too quickly:

> the lines drawn would suggest some object and at once I would develop them to make it look like that object. It seemed almost as if, at these moments, one could not bear the chaos and uncertainty about what was emerging long enough, as if one had to turn the scribble into some recognizable whole when in fact the thought or mood seeking expression had not yet reached that stage. And the result was a sense of false certainty, a compulsive and deceptive sanity, a tyrannical victory of the common sense view which always sees objects as objects, but at the cost of something else that was seeking recognition, something more to do with imaginative than common sense reality. (Quoted in Phillips 2000: 71)

A "compulsive and deceptive sanity" forces one to box up the world so as to make it intelligible and the price we pay is a deceptive oversimplification. Underlying our perceptual grip on the world is an exquisitely calibrated system of great skill and complexity. This susceptibility to being locked into a certain way of seeing, *despite our contrary knowledge*, can apply to a broader set of illusions that shape how we think about the world and each other.

Cognitive illusions

What is true of our perceptions is to some extent true of our reasoning skills. The analogy is not perfect since our habits of reasoning are more complex, holistic and alterable than our perceptual faculties.

Nonetheless the metaphor of the optical illusion as applied to higher realms of thought is quite fruitful in understanding the capacity to deceive ourselves and cook the facts. We are ill suited to inconsistency, loose ends, ambiguity and vagueness, and have heuristics and rules of thumb enabling us to be good problem-solvers. But these strengths are weaknesses too. When we don't find good answers to our questions we'll find others that do just as well. In looking to explain we can over-reach and superstitiously attribute causal links, like the gambler whose fallacy it is to believe that the amount of good luck she is due is linked to the amount of bad luck that preceded it.

This gift, and weakness, for explanation ignores the warnings of philosophers since David Hume, who observe the crucial difference between causation and correlation; namely, that when two events coincide it does not follow that one caused the other. In big cities the number of children born correlates better with the number of storks around than the amount of sex people have. This doesn't mean that the storybooks are right — babies aren't delivered by storks — it is just that when so much sex is non-procreative the correlation is low. Similarly ice cream doesn't cause skin cancer, although the two reliably correlate with each other (because sunshine influences them both). Yet we are very, very prone to making the fallacy; *post hoc ergo propter hoc* (after this therefore because of this). We use "fast and frugal" judgements to create simple and inevitably distorting pictures of the relationships between cause and effect. Companies routinely pay a huge bonus to the company director who arrives just in time to announce record profits (despite this being the culmination of years of work). Juries need to be sternly reminded that the defendant is innocent until proved guilty and that circumstantial evidence is insufficient to convict, in order to override (temporarily) the powerful tendency to feel that "there's no smoke without fire".

Human beings have an array of "biases and heuristics" that enable rough and ready calculations of stupendous complexity in a very short time, but the process is quite different from a logical weighing of evidence and marching deductively to the conclusion. Take the following description:

> Linda is thirty-one years old, single, outspoken and very bright. She studied philosophy. As a student, she was deeply concerned with issues of discrimination and social justice, and also participated in anti-nuclear demonstrations.

Now which of the following statements is more likely?

> A. Linda is a bank teller.
> B. Linda is a bank teller and is active in the feminist movement.

More than 85 per cent of people tested say that B is more likely than A. (The original experiment by Daniel Kahneman and Amos Tversky [1983] was more difficult because the two statements were embedded in a distracting group of eight.) With a moment's thought you can see that it cannot be that way around since the population of feminist bank tellers must be a subset of the broader population of bank tellers. So why did the subjects get it wrong? Because they were suckered by the description and assumed that all the information provided was *relevant* to Linda's career. The paleontologist and science writer Stephen Jay Gould wrote that he was particularly fond of this example because even though he knew (after it had been explained) that B is less likely than A, "a little homunculus inside my head continues to jump up and down, shouting at me – 'but she can't just be a bank teller; read the description'" (1991: 469). We are often, strictly speaking, *illogical* in our efforts to be *reasonable*.

We can look at the limits of imagination in a quite literal way. If you folded a very large piece of paper fifty times over how high would the stack become? One foot high? Ten feet? The actual answer is something like the distance from the earth to the sun (fourteen folds gets you to the average height of a man). One more fold and it would reach from here to the sun and back. In fact it is impossible to fold paper more than seven or eight times, but this thought experiment helps show our inability to visualize the power of geometric progression, like the ancient king who unwittingly handed over his kingdom by agreeing to the beggar's request for a grain of rice on the first square of a chess board, then two on the second, four on the third, eight on the fourth and so on. The king, like the rest of us, finds it difficult to imagine because he depended on "anchors" of information to gauge the suitability of a ballpark answer. In this case, extrapolating from the very small impedes his ability to visualize the very big.

The sheer range of deceptively simple rules of thumb that guide our interactions with the world is breathtaking; psychological research has identified more than a hundred ways one can bend the truth. We have a "hindsight bias" (I knew it all along), a "confirmation bias" (finding what we're looking for), an "availability bias" (over-stating the significance of vivid events); we find patterns in random shapes and conjure up a deceptive continuity despite the obvious fact of change. And these have serious societal implications. The ease with which concrete, vivid, recent information can be brought to mind affects our capacity for a moral response; this has found revolting expression in the remark usually attributed to Stalin that one death is a tragedy but a million deaths are a mere statistic. And despite Martin Amis's attempted rebuttal in *Koba the Dread* that "a million deaths are, at the very least, a million tragedies", charities have long recognized it is far more effective to engage us with a story of the suffering of a single child than to ask us to remember the 27,000 who die each day. To get from one to 27,000, let alone a million, is as hard as reaching the sun with folded paper. We can do it, sort of, but only by overriding the illusions that hold sway over us (and we cannot do that for long).

When we take together this bundle of techniques for making sense of the world we get a glimpse of how hard it is to unpack our common-sense judgements. We can begin to get some understanding of why people believe in astrology despite a scientific consensus that it is false, or buy lottery tickets at odds of 14,000,000 to 1, or why 46 per cent of people in the US believe the earth was created by God in the last 10,000 years. So our evolutionary inheritance, while giving us the skills we use to navigate our way through our social environments, gives us very little capacity for self-understanding. We can delude ourselves with great ease, especially when the temptation to console ourselves is high.

Narrative illusions

Homo credens is above all a storytelling animal. We understand what reality is, who we are, and how we ought to live by placing ourselves within the larger narratives and meta-narratives that we tell and hear, and that constitute for us what is real and significant. The philosopher Daniel Dennett comments in his book *Consciousness Explained* that "our fundamental tactic of self-protection, self-control and self-definition is not spinning webs or building dams, but telling stories, and more particularly concocting and controlling the story we tell others – and ourselves – about who we are" (1993: 418). The stories we need to tell explain the context in which action, intention and motivation are to be understood.

The child's question "Why?" reverberates throughout our lives and *demands* the response "Because …". Whether it is "it's my nature", "it's God's will" or "the sky is high", as long as *something* fills in the blank in order to provide the semblance of an answer we begin to relax. People love the word "because" to such an extent that it can soothe even when the explanation is empty of content. A famous study by psychologist Ellen Langer illustrates this point nicely. In this experiment the researcher approaches people queuing at a photocopier and asks "Can I get ahead of you?" to which the typical answer is no. But when the same request is made with the rider "because I need to make some copies", the answer tends to be yes. This non-explanation does its rhetorical work by dint of its form not its content. It uses the word "because" and hence *sounds* like an explanation, and the fact that it says nothing new seems strangely irrelevant. It is deeply ingrained in people to ask why and to reach (and over-reach) for "because". This readiness for meaning is in our grain.

We are profoundly attracted to illusory explanations that impute motives in the same way. Someone will angrily kick away the rock that lands on her foot as though it did it "on purpose". Picture Basil Fawlty manically giving his red Austen Morris "a damned good thrashing" in the middle of the road, for constantly stalling during his rush back to *Fawlty Towers* to rescue his doomed gourmet night. This tendency is so well developed that when shown a couple of dots moving about on a screen (on either side of a line) people routinely impute motives to them: one dot is trying to get in, one is trying to escape.

"Fawlty" thinking runs deep. We are helplessly teleological as we try to place a meaningful pattern on pointless occurrences; things seem to us to happen "for a reason" or, if not, simply "weren't meant to be", as though ordained by the stars, or the ubiquitous "they". Sometimes "they" need to be invoked, of course, when we are analysing the effect powerful people and institutions have on our lives, but the more common conversational usage of "they" has no particular target in mind (as in "Why don't *they* do something about … [fill in the blank]?!"). We are "wired" to see meaning in random events; cock-ups become conspiracies, we give thanks when things go well, or say we were born under an unlucky star when they don't. We have a special talent for invoking external and internal agents, fate, karma, cosmic energy, as a substitute for humdrum luck and judgement, and thus create the illusion that we have no say in the matter.

Alongside re-describing correlation as causation, imputing motives to mindless entities, we fall for an even more pernicious narrative illusion: ignoring the context. There is a very strong tendency to explain other people's behaviour by virtue of their supposed internal characteristics rather than the external forces that are in play. Let us return, briefly, to perceptual illusions to show what I mean. If you imagine dropping something from a plane the tendency is to think that it will fall straight down and to neglect the fact that rapid forward motion means that it will fall in an arc and land literally miles away from the point at which it was dropped. This is because people focus on the thing being dropped and massively discount the context in which the action takes place. Air force bombers, for example, have to be trained to override these intuitions and drop their payload well in advance of their target. Similarly, professional golfers on a sloped putting green deliberately putt wide of the mark as it appears to them, because they can't quite make themselves believe how far wide of the hole they have to go in order to account for the slope sufficiently.

This perceptual artefact has a powerful analogue when it comes to narrative illusions. The philosopher Gilbert Harman links this perceptual problem of focusing on the figure and ignoring the ground to a broader narrative problem known as the "fundamental attribution error". This error describes a tendency, when explaining others' behaviour, to overstate putative internal features (personality traits, inherent beliefs), while underestimating the impact of external features such as social context and situation. The last time you were cut up by another driver in traffic did you think "What a total idiot" or "He's in a hurry; must be important"? If, like most people, the former, then you were making a typical fundamental attribution error. We are more forgiving when explaining ourselves, of course.

The prevalence of this error means that if someone finds a wallet on the pavement and hands it in she does so, we tend to think, *because* she is honest (if she pockets the money first she does so *because* she is dishonest). Yet, as Harman points out, basic textbooks routinely explain that this is a very impoverished picture, since:

> there is surprisingly little consistency in people's friendliness, honesty, or any other personality trait from one situation to other, different situations. ... we often fail to realize this, and tend to assume that behavior is far more consistent and predictable than it really is. As a result, when we observe people's behavior, we jump to conclusions about their underlying personality far too readily and have much more confidence than we should in our ability to predict their behavior in other settings. (2003, quoting Kunda 1999: 395)

And we do this as part of evaluating them in the round. "Can I count on him when the heat is on?"; "Is she 'one of us'?"; at the core of these questions is whether we can believe the stories they tell us – can we trust them? And whether we can depends on their having comfortingly enduring traits that hold up: for better or worse, for richer or poorer, in sickness and in health. It is very easy to underestimate the fragile reliance on context of such traits, or of personality and character (until we see a film like *Trading Places*, which swapped the fates of a Dan Ackroyd's stockbroker for Eddie Murphy's conman – turning the first into a criminal and the second into a pillar of the community).

But to recognize our susceptibility to these narrative illusions, just as for the optical and cognitive kind, is not to override them. A health warning to remember is that while we may be able to think our way past these tendencies for a while, they regularly snap us back to square one. Crucially, for narrative illusions to work they need, as with perceptual and cognitive illusions, to be largely unconscious despite the enormous skill and concealed effort that makes them possible. Dennett describes this well:

and just as spiders don't have to think, consciously and deliberately, about how to spin their webs, and just as beavers, unlike professional human engineers, do not consciously and deliberately plan the structures they build, we (unlike professional storytellers) do not consciously and deliberately figure out what narratives to tell and how to tell them. Our tales are spun, but we for the most part don't spin them; they spin us. Our human consciousness, and our narrative selfhood, is their product, not their source. (1993: 418)

The evidence that our consciousness is merely the tip of a mental iceberg is overwhelming but hard to identify in everyday examples. What we call instinct, gut feeling or intuition is just a reflection of the fact that we know far more than we can tell. For example, doctors routinely disguise the amounts of intuition they use because it doesn't sound enough to say "the patient just didn't look right", even though this kind of reaction is usually what determines their "clinical judgement", more so than the list of symptoms they enumerate to confirm it. By definition, we can't be aware of the factors that have been pushed outside our awareness.

There is a more sinister reason why our stories need to be unconscious. In order to function in social groups we evolved to care about seeming trustworthy. *Homo credens* could not function without credit or credibility. Yet our needs and wants often conflict with the persuasive messages we need to convey: the office worker conceals his loathing of the boss; the faithful wife hides how much she fantasizes about her tennis coach. But lying deliberately can be difficult, stressful and easily detected, so the best liars have already convinced themselves. David Livingstone Smith, in his recent book *Why We Lie*, points out how:

The ability to harness the magic of words, and the capacity for self-deception that came in its wake, reconfigured the human psyche. In order to hide the truth about ourselves from ourselves, we needed to evolve an unconscious mind ... There is a side of ourselves that we were evolved not to know.   (2004: 3–4)

Natural born lie-detectors

The techniques of meaning-making discussed above make for unreliable sleuths. We leap to conclusions too easily. People have a tremendous appetite for revelation, for uncovering the secret. They look for concealment and get great satisfaction from solving the mystery, spotting the clue; and then are very prone to believing what has been uncovered. More generally, humans have evolved to care deeply about being convincing while being hard to convince: wanting to be believed while having an ear for the false note.

Why is deception and the fear of being deceived so central to human experience? It is as though our proneness to illusions, and jumping to conclusions, brings with it the uneasy thought that we are easily fooled. It is striking just how often our preoccupations are to do with appearance versus reality. The telltale cues are ubiquitous: "Do you really mean it?", "It's not what you think", "No, no, it's fine", "I'm not being funny but ...". We talk in richly layered code and are busily decoding at equal speed.

To understand this phenomenon well the cartoon cut-out of crude Darwinism needs to be displaced with a richer understanding of our so called "wiring". The reason humans are not driven purely to satisfy the four Fs (feeding, fighting, fleeing and sex) that drive all other animals is that they have evolved to be truly social. Contrary to prevalent misunderstandings about "selfish genes", evolutionary psychologists claim that our ancestors discovered that helping others can be a better survival strategy than helping yourself, on the Benjamin Franklin principle that "we must indeed all hang together, or, most assuredly, we shall all hang separately". Dennett has coined the term "benselfishness", in a nod to Franklin, to describe this concept of enlightened self-interest. For Dennett true altruism is a step further than this and can also be accounted for in Darwinian terms (see Chapter 7 of *Freedom Evolves* [2004] for the detail of his argument). This capacity for "reciprocal altruism" is as deeply ingrained in us as the other basic instincts.

Yet, if you picture these altruistic social groups of the Pleistocene era, innocently cooperating, you will realize that a widespread preference for generosity in a community is in turn the perfect breeding ground, so to speak, for cheats to emerge. And the threats posed by these "free riders", who pretend to be cooperators, create the need to catch them out, which then leads to the conditions under which finely tuned "cheater detectors" could have evolved. This is the evolutionist's claim. We are all now cheater detectors on some level. We can't stand to be made a mug of because, in the distant past, naive trust could have been lethal to our chances of survival. So we punish cheats, even if it costs us to do so. Economists who do not factor this in are baffled by the results of the ultimatum game, which involves two individuals who have never met before (call them Scorpion and Frog) sharing out money. Scorpion receives £10 and can choose how much to give to Frog. Frog can then decide to accept the offer or reject the whole deal (thus depriving Scorpion of any money too). Experiments show that if Scorpion gives Frog less than £4 she will reject the whole deal, even though *Homo economicus* should technically accept even £1 (since this is better than nothing). But *Homo credens* doesn't work that way, and doesn't like to be dissed.

We don't like cheats and deceivers and continually probe the appearance of sincerity by looking for the underlying motive; thinking "how *very* convenient" or "he would say that wouldn't he?" before deciding we will give the benefit of the doubt. As the psychologist Paul Ekman has shown, we can spot a fake smile in a moment if the groupings of forty-three distinct facial muscles (especially those around the eyes) don't contract in the right way. We have had to develop increasingly sophisticated mechanisms for being persuasive and assessing other's persuasiveness; because a reputation for being a good actor is immensely valuable in social groups. Specialists in this field often talk of an "arms race" of evolutionary moves and counter-measures leading up to the sheer complexity of society as we see it.

The psychologist Leda Cosmides (1989) has found remarkably vivid evidence of a built-in "cheater detection module". She took her starting-point from a famous series of experiments by Peter Wason in the early 1970s that were supposed to show the limits of rationality in human reasoning. The experimenter would give people four cards (each with a letter on one side and number on the other), the first and second with the letter facing up and the third and fourth with the number showing, as follows:

| D | F | 3 | 7 |

People were then asked to turn over the fewest cards necessary to test the rule "If a card shows a D then it has a 3 on the other side". Try it. If you are like most people (over 90 per cent of us) you will be inclined to turn over the D and the 3. The correct answer however, which almost nobody gets right, is to turn over the D and the 7, because turning over the 3 doesn't say anything about the rule "If there's a D then there's a 3"; that is, the rule does not require the reverse to be true. But if there's a D on the other side of the 7 the rule is false. We use practical inductive reasoning while the test demands a strict deductive approach.

This is a very well-established result in cognitive psychology. Cosmides decided to move the experiment out of the abstract into a real-life situation. In her version she says that you are a bouncer in a bar and you need to enforce the rule "If people are drinking beer they must be over 21". You are confronted with cards describing four people; on one side of each card you are given their age, and on the other what they are drinking. You are now asked to check the fewest number of cards needed to enforce the rule. Who do you check?

| Beer drinker | Coke drinker | 27 years old | 16 years old |

In this situation people pretty easily decide you need to check the first and the fourth person to enforce the rule. The suspicious barman in us will check how old the beer drinker is and will check what the teenager is drinking – almost automatically. The logic in both cases is the same and yet people can solve this problem far more easily than the abstract version. About 90 per cent of people get this version right.

But this is where things get interesting. Give the subjects another real-world situation (e.g. if someone eats hot chilli pepper then they must drink beer) and they get the answer wrong again. Concrete familiarity as opposed to abstraction is not the key to our improved performance; there is something else going on. Fascinatingly, it seems the difference in our ability to solve the problem comes only in a scenario where someone is breaching the rules of fair social exchange, that is, cheating. Mother nature, according to Cosmides, has installed in us "Darwinian algorithms" that are better suited for solving these problems than other cultural artefacts (such as formal logic, statistics, etc.). This striking result has been tested in different settings and holds up well. The correct interpretation of this data is debated, of course (by the philosopher David Buller, for example, in his book *Adapting Minds*), but it is good support for the claim that we are wired for detecting deception.

Reading minds

It is striking how often people feel the need to emphasize a point with phrases such as "I swear to God", "on my mother's life", "cross my heart and hope to die" or, less luridly, "if I'm honest, I have to say", "to tell you the truth", "if I can speak frankly" and "this time I really mean it" in an attempt to switch off the lie detectors. These verbal reassurances are attempts to say "please believe me" and "for all your understandable doubts, you can trust me on this one". But the reassurances aren't all that reassuring and often raise suspicions for two reasons. First, if you were honest in general why would you need to say so in this case? Second, words are cheap; it takes more than mere assertions to gain the credit you seek. To get a grip on the truth people need to look beyond what is said and hunt out the motive.

We have developed some useful techniques to detect the insincere. For example, one reason we are such avid consumers of gossip is that we learn about how consistently people act when we are not around and are therefore better placed to assess how what they do lines up with what they say. Moreover our appetite for meaning and persuasion sets us on the road to interpretation whenever our expectations are violated. We read minds. When we are confused by how someone is behaving we turn into a cross between Sherlock Holmes and an anthropologist as we work out what the devil is going on. If a man goes from door to door down a residential street wearing a uniform and pushing envelopes into letterboxes we don't think twice. If instead he's wearing jeans and a t-shirt and is looking through the letter boxes we start to look for explanations of what could be going on. What does he want? Is he a burglar looking for empty houses to rob? But why is he doing it in the cold light of day? What is he up to? What's his game? Maybe he's an over-zealous off-duty postman making sure his colleagues are doing their jobs.

We deploy our interpretative skills until we have come up with a reasonable account that makes behaviour intelligible. This is what Dennett calls adopting the "intentional stance". He contrasts making sense of people's behaviour with that of machines. In interpreting a thermometer it is enough to adopt the "design stance" to predict that when the temperature goes up, so does the mercury. That's what the mechanism was designed to do; once we know that we can predict its behaviour. When it comes to predicting other people we need to use the intentional stance to attribute what philosophers call "propositional attitudes", that is, a combination of beliefs and desires without which we would have no chance of understanding the behaviour in question. So we routinely explain someone's behaviour (getting up early, turning down a slice of cake) by guessing what she *desires* (to get to work on time, to lose weight) and what she *believes* (rush hour takes ages, cake makes you fat).

The key test of whether you truly have this mind-reading skill is revealed in your ability to attribute *false* beliefs to someone else. You predict that Jane will get up early on Monday, even though it is a bank holiday, because you know *she doesn't know* that. Simple as it seems to put yourself in Jane's shoes, this is quite a significant achievement as shown by a clever experiment known as the false belief test. Put a three-year-old child in a room and ask him to watch his mother as she hides a toy under a table. Then, after she leaves the room, take the toy from under the table and show her son that you've put it in a cupboard. When the mother returns to the room ask the child where she will look for the toy. The three-year-old, showing a touching faith in his mother's omniscience, will always get it wrong and say "in the cupboard". It is only when he is four and older that he will think to say "under the table", that is, where she last saw it. The four-year-old has developed the "theory of mind" that enables him to see things from her perspective, and only then can he attribute a false belief to her. And once we can see how people can entertain false beliefs, we gain the capacity to deceive them, and learn in turn that they might deceive us.

Of course in order to assess whether someone is a knave making fools of us we need to go beyond their words or even their deeds to be sure. We need more reliable clues to reveal their motives. Ekman says that one per cent of people are particularly gifted lie detectors because they notice the micro-expressions on faces that most of us miss, or only pick up unconsciously. Poker players work hard to identify "tells": the little uncontrollable signs (blink rates, sweating) that might be hints that someone is bluffing. The expression "a poker face" describes an attempt to fool mind readers, which is why poker experts are said to "play the player". And knowing this their equally skilled opponents create false "tells", such as scratching an ear apparently nervously, to throw opponents off the scent. The opponent needs to assess which of the leaky stream of "tells" provides a genuine clue. The most reliable clues, or at least those we latch on to most readily, are to do with the relevant display of emotion.

The biology of persuasion

We are not designed to seek the truth (about the world or ourselves) but to create meaning and to persuade each other of our versions. We scrutinize others' "genuine" claims and attempt equally to persuade others of our own. We want to trust and we want to appear trustworthy. With all this cheater-detection machinery humming in the background we need to be armed with mechanisms of persuasion.

Our emotions, the capacity for hatred, guilt, joy, love, anger, disgust and so on play a key role in enabling us to believe each other. We distrust people whose emotional range seems out of place with the situation at hand. Imagine that the scorpion was remorseful after killing the frog. How would he convince us that he did indeed regret his action? Does he offer a cool formal apology, or weep and wail? "Does he really mean it?" we ask. Too cool a response makes us suspicious, but equally we might find the "sackcloth and ashes bit" as "protesting too much". Appropriate emotional cues are the key to this. And while we learn much about how to deploy emotions (big boys learn not to cry), the sheer fact that we have them ties into the picture I want to paint of our being wired for belief and persuasion.

Evolutionary psychologists have neatly reverse engineered our basic emotional range and proposed them as evolved solutions to commitment problems, with their *involuntary* nature being a key feature of our credibility. Take anger as an example. Why in the world would anything as costly as a tendency to lose your temper ever have evolved? It is, after all, such a self-destructive emotion. In *How the Mind Works*, Pinker explains that it works like the Doomsday Machine in the film *Dr Strangelove*. The machine is a weapon designed by the Soviets during the cold war that is able to destroy all life on earth, and is *automatically* triggered by an enemy attack. The automatic nature of the response is key. The Doomsday Machine is the ultimate deterrent because even the fear of mutually assured destruction won't protect you from retaliation, so you'd better not provoke that automatic response. A rational approach when carrying out your threat to set off the machine might lead you to backing down for fear of harming yourself, and the very possibility that you might think twice about retaliating undermines the effectiveness of the threat in the first place.

The doomsday machine of rage avoids this problem by making retaliation *automatic* – without a second thought – so even the fear of self-destruction cannot stop you, figuratively speaking, from launching your missiles. A narrowly rational assessment of cost and benefit might be "it's not worth it", but on a wider view losing one's temper means you will do the irrational thing even if it proves self-damaging, and thus helps ensure aggressors steer clear of you in the first place. One definition of integrity is that someone does the right thing even if it hurts; well, so it goes for believing someone's threats.

Not only do emotions need to be automatic and hard to fake to be convincing, but they need to be detectable signals of our intent. If only the baddies in the television series *The Incredible Hulk* knew, in the first place, that the unprepossessing David Banner couldn't help becoming so shirt-splittingly mean and green they would have left him alone. This would have saved him the trouble of beating them up, revealing his secret identity and so having to run away and start all over again. As Dr Strangelove exclaimed to the Russian ambassador, "The whole point of having a Doomsday Machine is lost if you keep it a secret. Why didn't you tell the world?" If the Hulk could have conveyed his capacity for rage a little more effectively than saying "You won't like me when I'm angry", he could have saved us all that trouble. This is why, according to evolutionary theory, we wear the signs of our emotions on our faces, our hearts on our sleeves. We cry, we go red (rather than green), we sweat, we tremble, all as ways to communicate our emotional state, and thus persuade others to believe that "we really mean it".

Another surprisingly useful emotion is guilt, surprising because one might think guilt imposes an unnecessary constraint on helping oneself. Surely the free riders unencumbered by such distracting constraints will be able to ride all the more freely. Scruples are costly and so, one might think, should have died out. The economist Robert Frank found himself wondering why he gave tips to waiters in restaurants he would never be visiting again (on a business trip for example). Why not just sign the bill, add the tip and leave? On a utility model he should be expecting something in return for a tip, but since he wasn't going to be a repeat customer, or even see the waiter again after paying, he was at a loss to explain what – except that he didn't want to feel guilty for short changing the waiter.

Frank suggests that this costly adaptation could have improved the chance of survival for a truly social animal. The simple reason being that people who are known to have a conscience are more easily trusted and benefits accrue to those who are trusted. Your capacity for guilt helps you come across as the kind of person for whom a promise is a promise. The prisoner's dilemma works better for both parties if they trust each other enough not to snitch. Now, one might argue that it is just enough to *come across* as capable of feeling guilty in order to *seem* trustworthy. Why not just fake a conscience? And people do try, no doubt; but this is easier said than done. If emotions were easy to fake they would be less potent sources of credibility. Our intuitive, unconscious assessment picks up on the slightest sign that emotion tone is off. And even though people try to fake guilt, the audience has a well-honed cheater-detection mechanism to spot the effort. As Frank concludes in *Passions within Reason*, it appears the best way to *seem* good is actually to *be* good.

Love, similarly is claimed to have evolved for solving these "commitment problems". Contrary to the Darwinian cliché, people regularly fall in love by flouting the rules of good genetic stock maintenance. Love isn't instrumental. Like anger and guilt, it is an *irrational* leap that guarantees our sincerity. This is why it is said that people who are sensible about love are incapable of it. This fact is also very costly, as anyone who has known the anguish of unrequited love will testify. So why, again, would such a costly emotion have evolved? Pinker explains how this can be so:

> Somewhere in the world of five billion people there lives the best-looking, richest, smartest, funniest, kindest person who would settle for you. But your dreamboat is a needle in a haystack, and you may die single if you wait for him or her to show up ... At some point it pays to set up house with the best person you have found so far.   (Pinker 1998: 417)

But this cold calculus leaves your partner extremely vulnerable. "The laws of probability say that some day you will meet a more desirable person, and if you are always going for the best you can get, on that day you will dump your partner" (*ibid.*). This, according to evolutionary psychology is why romantic love might have evolved. It works as a guarantee that the person who has settled for you has not done so tactically, ready to drop you at the first sign of a better prospect. They chose you because they have fallen for something distinctively you: the shape of your nose, the way you walk, your sense of humour. Thus the irrationality of falling madly in love (as the songs and films insist, "You drive me crazy", "I can't help loving you") is the evolutionary key that opens the door to *true* love.

In the case of anger, guilt or love we can see how we have evolved mechanisms that enable us to be persuasive in a community of doubters, and jumpers to conclusions. The intellect, as Pinker says, "is designed to relinquish control to the passions so that they may serve as guarantors of its offers, promises, and threats against suspicions that they are lowballs, double-crosses and bluffs" (*ibid.*).

While emotions help to convey sincerity because they are hard to control they are, paradoxically, also a classic motor for deception and self-deception. Whether enraged, full of guilt or madly in love, the presence of strong emotion tends to create a colourful filter through which to interpret the world and other people. Stendhal describes the "crystallization" that comes from loving, for instance, as "that action of the mind that discovers fresh perfections in its beloved at every turn of events". The presence of emotion also invites a *post hoc* explanation that may have nothing to do with why it was conjured up in the first place. The husband angry with his wife because she reminds him of his mother is liable to pick a convenient alternative explanation to account for his behaviour. The centrality of emotion to our capacity for credibility and deception runs through this book.

Explaining ourselves

The need to separate appearance from reality and to make sense of the world is fundamental to human nature, leaving *Homo credens* in an eternal struggle over what to believe. We may, along with all other animals, have evolved the bodies and perceptual facilities to put order on the chaos of experience but, more than any other animal, things got complicated for us and in order to flourish in early social settings we evolved mechanisms for interaction that set us on a spiral of increasing complexity. At heart humans have to simplify and have to convince by telling stories that conceal from view the ragged-edged complexity of the world and ourselves. We cook up our versions, conceal limitations from view, while trying to get them past our own and each others' deception detectors. The prize for getting our story to hold up is a simpler, more predictable world in which we feel relatively blameless and competent.

People are discomfited by uncertainty and suffer a fear of the open-ended and messy details of life, alongside a deep need to be sure. They gravitate around individuals who appear sure of themselves (until confidence turns into arrogance at least), and are brought low by a sense of meaninglessness, consoling themselves with simple-minded recipes, consuming varieties of chicken soup for the soul spooned into them by gurus, politicians, journalists and priests. The seven steps to eternal happiness vie with the ten commandments to tidy up a modern identity, and to leave difficult questions to one side. We have evolved to want quick and simple answers: "closures" that shut down those questions, whether provided by a higher power, an inner child or a tabloid horoscope.

Take the simple question: why did I do that? We tend not to ask it when things are going well, but often when there is cause to regret. We ask it of ourselves when we've stayed up too late despite having to get up early for a job interview; or gushed when trying to be cool; when we've said something hurtful to the one we love; when

33

we've taken a crazy risk; or not said what we'd planned to … again! The scorpion might have asked it as he was drowning. Thanks to the easy lure of the fundamental attribution error, when describing someone else we can use an incurious shorthand: why did he do that? Oh, he's just "wired" that way; boys will be boys; he's basically a chip off the old block; and a typical Capricorn, not to mention the jealous type; his parents split up when he was young; it's tradition anyway; after all he's Dutch; it's in his nature.

But this simple question offers a way, if we make the effort to answer it well, into the layers of human and societal complexity that lie behind the illusions of coherence, order, singularity, sanity that we like and need to maintain for ourselves. *Why did I do that?* An unending search for a more honest answer takes us past the creeping exculpation of the scorpion through memory (What actually happened?), will power (Could I have done differently?), identity (Am I the person I thought I was?), justification (How can I feel OK about what I did?), meaning (It's not what you think), reputation (What will they think of me now?), accountability (It's not my fault) and relevance (That's not the point), and honesty, bad faith, integrity, social technique, mixed motives and self-deception all play a part.

Beyond these attempts to look for the springs of action within, it is equally important to look at the culture and context in which we act. The invisible ethical climate that we inhabit is like the impact of a speeding plane on a bomb being dropped. Take cheating. It is clear that we are skilled deceivers and detectors of deceit and that when trust breaks down so do many social arrangements and self-denying conventions. After all it doesn't make much sense to keep your place standing in a queue when everyone else has rushed to the front. So when we see, as the political scientist Bo Rothstein has shown, that the tax take in Russia is 26 per cent of what it should be if everyone paid their taxes, while the equivalent number in Sweden is 95 per cent, we had better look for much more than a "cheater-detection module" to understand the conditions under which beliefs in some cultural institutions hold up while in others they break down.

As should be obvious now, the reason it is so difficult to resist consolations and deceptive illusions is to do with the fact that most of our mental processes are hidden from view and designed to stay that way. Most thinking we do is unconscious, hiding contradictions, and this is necessary to acting well and convincingly in pursuit of our goals. The next chapter explores these subtleties of self-deception in more depth.

2. Deceiving ourselves: you can't always know what you want

Every man has reminiscences which he would not tell to everyone but only to his friends. He has other matters in his mind which he would not reveal even to his friends, but only to himself and that in secret. But there are other things a man is afraid to tell even to himself, and every decent man has a number of such things stored away in his mind.

(Dostoevsky, *Notes from the Underground*)

In Chapter 1 we saw how self-deception took root in the human mind so as to enable us to be better able to persuade others. These others, equipped with their cheater-detection skills, are well tuned to spot a phoney performance and so automatic, unconscious mechanisms become essential to our chances of being convincing. The most convincing storytellers believe their own stories, persuading themselves of their sanity, consistency, reasonableness and virtue. This requires that internal contradictions, what psychologists call cognitive dissonance, get neatly ironed out. Cognitive dissonance theory suggests that we confabulate when confronted with awkward knowledge (I know smoking can give me cancer) that clashes with behaviour (and yet I smoke) in order to alleviate the tension. The tension does not come simply from the fact of inconsistency; rather, it is triggered more broadly by threats to our reputation or self-image. As the psychologist Elliott Aronson (1980) concluded, we deceive ourselves specifically when confronted with evidence that we are not "nice and in control". Dissonance is triggered by evidence that you are not as well-motivated and competent as you would like people to think, and the need to reduce it is the unconscious need to explain that evidence away.

But isn't there something incoherent about the very idea of self-deception? If you are motivated to *deceive* yourself about some difficult issue (e.g. whether you should spend more time with your children), how can you possibly succeed unless you *know* what it is you have to deceive yourself about, in which case, does it make any sense to say you are actually deceived? How can I be both dupe and knave? Where contradictory desires meet self-deception we talk of being weak-willed: "I know this is what I should do, and yet I don't do it"; "I know I shouldn't but I can't help myself". Philosophers since antiquity have asked how it is possible to suffer from *akrasia*, the Greek term for incontinence (weakness of will rather than bladder!). A truly weak will, as opposed to hypocrisy or conventional dishonesty, seems on the face of it paradoxical. How can we act in ways that we know run against our considered judgement about what it is best to do? As Socrates puts it (in Plato's *Protagoras*, 352c) knowledge cannot "be pushed around by all the other affections". His over-optimistic conclusion is that "no one does wrong willingly", and so if people choose to act in a way that is cause for regret then they must have misjudged in the first place: we cannot judge something as not the best thing to do, and then do it. And yet we do! The novelist John Cheever's description of his alcoholism vividly represents this helplessness:

> year after year I read [in my journals] that I am drinking too much … I waste more days, I suffer deep pangs of guilt, I wake up at three in the morning with the feelings of a temperance worker. Drink, its implements, environments and effects all seem disgusting. And yet each noon I reach for the whiskey bottle. (1990: 29)

Cheever the temperance worker by night jostles alongside Cheever the alcoholic by day. This fact suggests that we cannot simply fuse these two into a single aggregate identity called John Cheever. Candidate explanations for this apparent irrationality involve the idea of "partitioning" distinct selves competing within us to promote their different priorities. In Freudian terms the Ego is not master in its own house because the rival (unconscious) Id is making mischief, and turning the tables, as evidenced by slips of the tongue, odd forgettings and exaggerated fears. In *Problems of Rationality* Donald Davidson takes seriously this suggestion by arguing that the Freudian unconscious mind is best seen as another person sharing the same brain with the conscious mind. There is the same coherence of belief and desire in the unconscious mind as there is in the conscious mind but the two are distinct from each other. The Freudian slip then is an irrational intrusion from the point of view of the conscious mind, but quite rational from the viewpoint of the unconscious (with its own coherent network of beliefs and desires). This, for Davidson is how it is possible to believe that p, and believe that not-p (without believing the irrational conjunction that p and not-p).

Despite Davidson's creative use of Freud to square the circle, the debates have continued down the ages and, unsurprisingly, the jury is still out on self-deception and weak will in the strictest sense. Whether or not true *akrasia* is logically possible, there is an undeniable empirical reality that we act in ways that run against our interests, our moral principles or long-term goals.

In this chapter I explore how much less nice or in control we are than we might like to appear and there is nothing more threatening to this self-serving image than unruly desire. Our short-term drives undermine our long-term aims, and what we feel we *ought to want* is starkly challenged by what we *really want*. When we glimpse our mixed motives we worry about our reliability and credibility; we warn each other about what happens to curious cats, and fear thin ends of slippery slopes. Conveniently our minds are equipped with mechanisms of self-delusion that keep reality at bay; our hindsight, foresight and insight are as systematically prone to narrative illusions as our eyesight is to the perceptual illusions described in Chapter 1, which, as we shall see, is why we are so bad at predicting what will satisfy us in future.

If we cannot wish our wishes away so easily, we must resort to telling coherent, credible tales to each other so as to smooth over complexity. We try to find a way to describe our motives so as to feel OK about the risks we have taken. In short, when confronted by the question "Why did I do that?", we must make our desires appear to be reasonable. In attempting to tease out the subtle themes of this chapter, namely the relationship between paradoxical desire and self-deception, the acute-eyed novelist (think of Flaubert writing *Madame Bovary*) can serve us well. I shall draw on a more contemporary source to help illustrate my themes; namely, Lionel Shriver's usefully searing novel *We Need to Talk about Kevin*.

Speaking the unspeakable about Kevin

In *Kevin* (as I shall refer to the novel), the narrator, Eva Khatchadourian, is writing letters to her estranged husband, Franklin, as a way to come to terms with the question "Why did he do that?" The *he* in question is their teenage son Kevin and the thing he did was a Columbine-style mass murder of nine people at his school (including seven fellow students). For obvious reasons these three characters, Eva, Franklin and Kevin, spectacularly fail to get what they wanted. More interestingly they illustrate well how our cognitively dissonant stories, the self-serving accounts of what needs we have and how we might meet them, can clash with each other: how we trade in honesty for hope.

As we read Eva's letters we discover much about the secret lives that underlie our normality. Flayed by this ghastly experience, the thin veneer of self-deception that normally shrouds her self-awareness is torn off and Eva starts to volunteer to her husband and the reader "those unutterable little truths" that she barely dared to think before: that she didn't like her son from the beginning and for years after; that she hated the expensive new house Franklin had bought as a surprise; that once "something wicked in me" wanted another man (during a boringly nice lunch with friends) to slip his hand up her skirt.

Eva recognizes that she is churlish and pessimistic while Franklin is presented as the smoothed over foil against which she can express her "cussedly non-specific dissatisfactions". He is suspicious of her complex version of the world and dismissive of what he deems her self-regarding cynicism, while leaving the reader to wince at his hair-ruffling, puppy love for his brooding and dangerous son. As the counterpoint to her complexity he has blithe optimism about his country (as an unflinchingly patriotic Republican) as well as his relationships with Eva and Kevin, and accuses Eva of moral snobbery. Franklin regards redemption as an act of will: "nice eats, nice place, nice folks – what more could I possibly want?" Chastened by him Eva sometimes berates herself for her "unformed" and "fleeting" disquiet. Yet, despite her occasional self-doubt, she diagnoses eloquently Franklin's deluded optimism as the "compulsion to manhandle your unruly misshapen experience into a tidy box, like someone trying to cram a wild tangle of driftwood into a hard-shell Samsonite suitcase". Contrary to the philosophical injunction that we can never get an "ought" from an "is", Eva can see that he (quite sincerely) confuses the two, describing it as "your heartrending tendency to mistake what you actually had for what you desperately wanted ...". The theme of this chapter could hardly be better expressed. This "compulsion" exists in us all, to some degree, and in Eva herself, of course; but as with beams and motes we are much better at identifying these tendencies in others than in ourselves.

In *Kevin* we have no difficulty seeing the gap between the father's simplistic perceptions and the cold reality of the son's psychology. While Franklin is buoyantly certain that Kevin is just an ordinary kid, Kevin is presented as completely the opposite of his father; so bleakly clear-eyed (and honest in a way) that he cannot see the point of anything or anyone. He has no idea why other people find anything precious. For him, all that they treasure is a sham, and the secret of adulthood is that there is no secret. Even in prison, after his act of savagery, his remorseless hostility is undimmed. He tells his mother to stop visiting:

> "You may be fooling the neighbours and the guards and Jesus and your gaga mother with these goody-goody visits of yours, but you're not fooling me. Keep it up if you want a gold star. But don't be dragging your ass back here on my account". He added, "because I hate you."

Eva realises this is no childish tantrum, but a gimlet-eyed assessment that forces an honesty on her part in return. She has by now been seasoned enough not to offer a cliché in response:

> I had some idea of what I was supposed to say back *Now, I know you don't mean that*, when I knew that he did. *Or I love you anyway, young man, whether you like it or not*. But I had an inkling that it was following just these pat scripts that helped to land me [in this mess]. So instead I said, in the same informational tone, "I often hate you too, Kevin" and turned heel.

The three characters in *Kevin* can stand as metaphors for how we handle the world with varying degrees of honesty and hope, how much we cling to or reject consolatory "pat scripts". Eva's ability to utter the unutterable is enabled, perversely, by the devastating blow she and her family have faced. It is almost as though we can only expect to be as honest as Kevin is throughout, and as Eva has become, when we feel we have absolutely nothing to lose. While on some level and to differing degrees Franklin, Eva and even the nihilistic Kevin all populate our densely rich psychology, by the very fact that we have much to lose (such as our reputations in the eyes of those who matter) we need to curb our self-scrutiny to some degree.

Yet the danger of averting our gaze too effectively is to end up like Franklin. Franklin is happier on the face of it, but has to work hard to avoid glimpsing his own vulnerability. He cannot but doubt his own version of their family life, on some level, in the light of his wife's potent gaze, and frequently gets angry with her. Franklin commits himself to picture-postcard smoothness, while Eva looks into the fractures and crags. She's the sour seer, the doubter, the anti-romantic, who makes Franklin look naive, but she is a storyteller too. And her highly intelligent son, who becomes a sociopath, can see through her cover-ups and self-exculpatory accounts; he does to her what she does to Franklin. Here he is responding to Eva's cheery preparations for Christmas. She patiently explains to her son that she is too sophisticated to believe in Christianity but that, as she learned while studying anthropology, "it's important to observe cultural rituals":

"Just so long as they're totally empty," said Kevin breezily.

"You think we're hypocrites."

"Your word, not mine." ...

"So," Kevin summed up ... "you want to keep the presents and the high-test eggnog, but chuck the prayers and the boring Chrismas Eve service. To cash in on the good stuff without having to pay for it with the shit."

"You could say that," I agreed cautiously. "In a broad sense I've tried to do that all my life."

43

"Okay, long as you can get away with it," he said cryptically. "Not sure it's always possible." And he let the subject go.

Only later do we see his vicious plan to make sure she doesn't get away with anything. And yet her crime, "to cash in on the good stuff without having to pay for it with the shit", is a commonplace ambition: something we have all tried to do on occasion.

So these three characters exist in us all. Franklin stands for idealization and self-deception and how these are used to create consolation prizes. Kevin, his nemesis, represents the inability to sustain a convenient fiction; like the depressed he looks bleakly at the world, unadorned by hope, and sees nothing of value in it. Eva represents endless conflict between hope and despair: honest enough (although not as bleakly honest as Kevin) to know she wants differing things at the same time; hopeful enough to invest in things and people around her, while clear-eyed enough to be disappointed, by herself and by others. Unlike Kevin, she wants to want things, but she shows us the dangers of self-scrutiny. If you look too hard you may not like what you find.

Mixed motives

What will not have been apparent from my version of *Kevin* above was just how deeply Eva loved Franklin. His strong simple grip on the half-full glass had a tempting solidity for her. She compares him to an oak tree providing the branches she can rest in, and depend on. Eva is surprised, and relieved, by the kind of man she fell in love with. She thought she wanted someone as crooked and subtle as herself but in fact is deeply grateful to have been wrong about this: "how lucky we are, when we're spared what we think we want". But the enduring, and unendurable, problem with our mongrel desires, the "unutterable little truth", is that we cannot want what we have.

The etymology of "want" is rooted in lack or absence. Those in want are needy (and full of unfulfilled desires) while those who want for nothing are impossible to buy birthday presents for. Desire depends on lack, or at least obstacles to its fulfilment.

And so, even as Eva swings from Franklin's branches, she gets too blithe and optimistic to settle for what she has. She wants more, and is tempted, fatefully, "to turn the page". Their next adventure is to have a child and even though she is doubtful of the merits in having children she is suckered by the purity of Franklin's love which: "made me greedy. Like an addict worth his salt, I wanted more. And I was curious ... You started it – like someone who gives you a gift of a single carved ebony elephant, and suddenly you get this idea that it might be fun to start a collection."

She dares to desire more, and it is in the logic of wanting more that one day ambition will fail. For her that day came when she met Kevin. When she gave birth to him she realized she had wanted:

> what I could not imagine. I wanted to be transformed: I wanted to be transported. I wanted a door to open and a whole new vista to expand before me that I had never known was out there. I wanted nothing short of revelation, and revelation by its nature cannot be anticipated, it promises that to which we are not yet privy ... expectations are dangerous when they are both high and unformed.

Like Eva we often find our desires surprisingly obscure and our hopes dangerous. What do we truly want? And why are we not easily satisfied? The psychoanalyst Adam Phillips in his recent book *Going Sane* reminds us of the infantile pleasures of "being loved, adored, stroked, held, cuddled, infinitely attended to and responded to, and thought about; of only sleeping, eating and playing", because these, according to Freud, are the truly satisfying pleasures. For Freud, says Phillips, ultimate happiness:

depends on our being able to carry on, however cunningly, meeting our prehistoric wishes … the sane adult is always smuggling his childhood into the future, refashioning his childhood pleasures as legitimate adult interests. And this means not being fooled about what these wishes actually were. (2005: 200)

But this is an overly sanitized version of adult sanity. Sex and money, for Phillips the two sets of desires that mark us off from children, at the very least complicate the picture. Sexuality, for instance, "plays havoc with our logic, with our just-so cause-and-effect stories, with our modern obsession with security in human relations and with our ability to make promises" (*ibid.*: 132).

The prehistoric wishes may persist but they are ancient shapes in a modern terrain; fused and blended with new styles presented to us by consumer culture. We want many things because we are told about them, even told to want them. With these cultural imperatives around us we become conformists who prefer what is preferred by others, or anti-conformists who shrug off those norms in search of novelty. Anti-conformists, of course, must monitor conventional preferences so as to be out of phase with them: negative slaves of fashion condemned to live in what my daughter Anna used to call "opposite-land". With our personalized number plates we traffic in an economy of desires that are not of our own making, and we are never truly satisfied because we do not know what to want:

[A]ll creatures are endangered by the fundamental project of meeting their needs. But the human creature meets his needs, in both senses, unlike every other animal. He must meet his needs in order to survive, and over time he will have to become acquainted, too, with what he will learn to call his needs. And what he will meet, unlike any other animal, is the exorbitance, the hubris of his appetites. Indeed the stories he will be told about his appetite – explicitly in words and implicitly in the way his appetite is responded to by other people – is that it is, at least potentially, way in excess of any object's capacity to satisfy.   (*Ibid.*)

Phillips reminds us of some of the reasons we cannot reasonably expect to meet our needs. Our "exorbitance" ensures we always want more than we can have; so much so that we often need to conceal our appetites from view if we are to seem nice and in control. Our passions, wishes, intentions, drives, motives, hopes, expectations, ambitions and desires pose a constant challenge to our self-image. They threaten the norms of normality and acceptability to which we must submit.

Our appetites are not just excessive and obscure but they conflict. In my book *The Happiness Paradox* I detail a central tension that runs through the story of human identity: that between the need to feel free and the need to feel justified. Torn by our contradictory desires, whether around food, sex, money, reputation, freedom or love and affection; we want to be normal *and* original, righteous *and* transgressive, fair-minded *and* fulfilled, honest *and* kind. We want to drink beer *and* to lose weight: genuinely. We are many people wanting many things and are forced to live one life in one body, and so struggle to explain the actions we regret but cannot resist. The ego is not master in its own house, says Freud, and this is more than a metaphor. Franklin, Eva and Kevin are competing within us, as are a number of other characters: some chasing love, others chasing money; some wanting curry, others wanting abs. The New Year's resolve to diet crashes at the first binge, leading to glutton's remorse and mass binning of all things sweet, then an expensive gym membership … until the next binge.

And when we fail we talk in a moralistic tone of having "let ourselves down", and promise to do "better next time". Salman Rushdie (in his advertising days) was clearly on to something when he called cream cakes "naughty but nice". At some point in developing from an impulsive child to a conflicted adult, *Homo credens* has learned that the price of a good reputation is putting away (or at least hiding) childish things. We need to feel justified – to ourselves and each other – and value a good reputation to such a high degree that we will bury short-term desires in its pursuit. Self-deception is crucial to our chances of success. Our preferred descriptions of ourselves as reliable, trustworthy, intelligible, kind, only stand up if we successfully avert our gaze from these unruly desires; hiding our deep-seated wishes from view is the price we pay for peace of mind. But self-deception does not solve the conflicts, it just disguises them.

Leaps of faith or playing safe

One of the key drivers of self-deception is the fear of looking a fool. We are careful about admitting to what we really like because our tastes are not quite the right shape for polite company. So we pretend that they are. No one likes to admit the envy that reveals secret wishes for more sex, recognition or money and the self-aggrandizing ugliness of "unrealistic ambitions". Our deceptive skills ensure that we protect our self-image. To fail to do so is to be heading for a fall. We frequently rationalize our choices after a disappointment and hope to seem reasonable in retrospect, regretting *rien*. If we can pull this off our face is saved. Sometimes, though, there is no convincing get-out clause. When we make the mistake of showing our unrequited desires at their full height we feel stigma and are forced to acknowledge our arrogance or naivety; "How could I have been so stupid?" we say, or "I feel a fool", "Who did I think I was kidding?" And to avoid this feeling of shame we put energy and skill into curtailing our secret ambitions and expect others to do the same. It is for this reason that Franklin's reckless optimism about his relationship with Kevin makes us cringe. It would be painfully funny to read if it weren't so tragic.

Take the tragedy out and you get a British television genre known as the "comedy of embarrassment". In the sitcom *Only Fools and Horses*, a classic of the type, the lead character, Del Boy, is in a yuppie wine bar with his friend Trigger eyeing up a couple of women. As the women begin to smile back, he tells his friend to "play it nice and cool" and leans back casually against a bar flap that has just been raised, unbeknown to him, behind his back. The pratfall as he tips out of shot, cocktail still in hand, is deservedly one of the great moments of television comedy, leaving the not-too-bright Trigger looking around mildly bemused that his friend has disappeared. The scene works as a painfully funny reminder of how easily our pretensions can be punctured, as when the pompous banker steps on the banana peel, or when Franklin gives his snide son an enthusiastic bear-hug. We wince, because their lack of self-protection makes us uneasily aware of our own vulnerability. Our credibility, if we overreach, can be pricked in a second and so we try not to drop our guard. The genius of the scene lies in the defence-lessness of both characters. When interviewed about it David Jason (who plays Del Boy) explains how as he falls back, almost in slow motion, he does nothing to break the fall. This is almost impossible to do. When people fall they automatically bend a knee or put a hand back to protect against the impact, but Del Boy just keeps on falling. Like a trusting child, or a drunk, he is not capable of even this elementary piece of self-protection. His vulnerability is all the more poignant for being in no way covered up; while the audience sees the risk to his dignity he is oblivious, as befits a man whose constant refrain is "Who dares wins". Unlike Del Boy, we usually find a way to break our fall and find ways to maintain our dignity and minimize any sense of shame.

In the safe places of much art, such as feel-good films and uplifting novels, the possibility of "happily ever after" is affirmed. And when life imitates that art, when we dare to hope and win, we, like Eva, get "hungry for more" and become ever more risky. The happiness of the lucky stands as a rebuke to those who have cramped their wishes to avoid disappointment: those who are playing safe with sour grapes. The lucky remind us of our braver selves, of the more innocent, younger selves that were in the ascendant before we learned the hard way. But some people never learn, and it is easy to be resentful or anxious about them; to see them as, like Del Boy, "riding for a fall" as they swing blithely from branch to branch of high expectations without fear. He doesn't know that he is constantly making a fool of himself, with his SAS mantra, and when it happens, when he dares and loses, like a cartoon character hit over the head with an mallet, he seems to bounce back every time. For most of us, each failure or embarrassment leaves a mark and teaches a lesson. Never wanting to be lambs to the slaughter, we shudder to imagine asking a Kevin (as Yeats asked his lover) to "Tread softly because you tread on my dreams". And like Eva, and unlike Del Boy, we trade innocence for experience.

What we want to want, or ought to want, competes with what we really want; we feel condemned to regretting our inability to resist temptation, take precautions, to be careful what we wish for, and keep ourselves busy. With our heads down we needn't become too "acquainted" with the fact that we have mixed motives and should sometimes fear our hopes. We hide them from ourselves quite successfully and in the process we become estranged from these desires. But every once in a while we can get glimpses of our wayward likes and dislikes, hopes and fears, such as when we are too quick to anger, or feel envious, or sexually excited, or ashamed, or when we dream (by day or night) or laugh nervously.

Take the last of these. Sometimes laughter covers up a desire to ridicule as much as to applaud; where laughing *with* someone shades into laughing *at* them. Michael Billig, in his deeply insightful book *Laughter and Ridicule*, points out that in close relationships teasing is often seen as much more amiable by the teaser than by the one being teased. The latter can hear the implicit mockery the teaser conceals from her own version of events. Why are the most potent jokes apt to create strong disapproval? In Billig's discussion of Freud's *Jokes and Their Relation to the Unconscious*, he shows why people laugh much harder at risqué, tendentious jokes (which break taboos about sex and aggression) than at innocent ones. We kid ourselves that we're laughing at the construction, the wit, the delivery and are less ready to admit we are titillated by the content and what that speaks to in ourselves. But our rationalization doesn't hold up on closer scrutiny. Both tendentious and innocent jokes have the same technical qualities in order to work as a joke in the first place, such as double-meanings and reversals of expectation, and can be told with equally good comic timing. So what can be the difference between the two kinds, where only the second creates gales of mirth? "[A] suspicion may be aroused in us that tendentious jokes, by virtue of their purpose, must have sources of pleasure at their disposal to which innocent jokes have no access" (Freud, quoted in Billig 2005: 157).

Laughter can police as well as release. We laugh sometimes as a form of social repair when a situation is getting out of hand, such as when someone is getting aggressive or too rude; sometimes a pun can puncture the atmosphere and punish the aggressor with a disguised punch for good measure. We do not understand well what wishes are being expressed when we laugh, which is why we should be sceptical of the person who tries to repair an offensive remark with "Come on, I'm only joking". They may well believe that they meant nothing by the comment, but this does not mean they did not. Their intent may well be concealed by self-deception.

Of course, much of the time we need to get by, to get on, and so these uneasy insights must be routinely obliterated with consolations and deceptions: boxed in with oversimplified, commonsensical stories about ourselves and each other. Our self-respect and self-trust depend on obscuring from view the fantasies and doubts that shadow our daily rhythm effectively enough to deny them with a clear conscience.

Fooling ourselves

Our minds are equipped with a convincing knack for cooking the facts, whether future, present or past. Take the psychologist Elizabeth Loftus, who was shocked to hear from her uncle that at the age of fourteen (thirty years earlier) she had been the one to find her mother's body in the pool in which she had drowned. She had until then not known much about her mother's death and certainly had no idea she had discovered the body. But soon after this revelation she began to remember the awful details:

> like the crisp, piney smoke from evening camp fires. My mother, dressed in her nightgown, was floating face down .... I started screaming. I remembered the police cars, their lights flashing. For three days my memory expanded and swelled. Then, early one morning, my brother called to tell me that my uncle had made a mistake. Now he remembered (and other relatives confirmed) that Aunt Pearl found my mother's body. (Quoted in Neimark 1995)

Ironically Loftus is an authority on human memory, and her research has shown how prone people are to constructing *post hoc* versions of events that never happened. "My own experiment had inadvertently been performed on me! I was left with a sense of wonder at the inherent credulity of even my sceptical mind."

Foresight is just as soaked in cooked facts as hindsight. We predict the future badly for the various reasons addressed already, but one obvious reason is that we are rash. We are impulsive, and will discount the future heavily when given the choice. That's why people are often negligent about their pension provision: what is close looms larger. When Franklin wanted to buy the house that Eva would come to hate, she was persuaded to support the move to the suburbs in exchange for just one more adventure (a three-month trip to Africa): "my deal was pretty raw but then desperate people will often opt for short-term relief in exchange for long-term losses. So I sold my birthright for a bowl of soup".

We may be rash and impulsive and discount the future, but this is far from the only reason that answered prayers can be so disappointing. We can't always get what we want because we so often mis-predict how we will feel about a future event when we get there. There is something unsettling about the word *dream*, as in dream holiday, dream wedding, dream job or Franklin's American dream, in that it invites us to create the *wish you were here* picture-postcard smoothness that is almost bound to be a caricature (and equally bound to be a disappointment).

In his recent book *Stumbling on Happiness*, the psychologist Daniel Gilbert has pulled together an enormously wide range of research to show why this is. He calls the significant mismatch between what we predict and what we end up experiencing an "impact bias", which leads us to make mistakes in choosing what we think will make us happy. We overestimate what we will enjoy and underestimate how well we will cope with feared outcomes (such as losing a job, divorce or becoming very ill) because the future is stranger and more complex than we allow. There are three reasons our imaginations looking into the future can be as easily fooled as our eyes looking into space: "realism", "presentism" and "rationalization".

Take realism first. Our imagination works so effortlessly, so transparently, that we are prone to believing its contents. We saw earlier with Loftus that when we remember we are often fabricating rather than merely retrieving the past, but the work is unconscious and rapid and so we feel like we are simply replaying a tape. The same goes for looking forwards in time. Imagine how you would feel if you were at the beach next week. Not only will you be able to do this with no effort at all, but you will have added many plausible details that were not implied in the task. Maybe you are with your family digging holes in the sand, or alone under a palm tree, sipping a drink and reading a book. Are you wearing a sarong or nothing at all? Are you sleeping or swimming? Are you in Spain or the Caribbean? The point is that you will effortlessly conjure up a detailed picture of this imagined future and call up myriad invented, but highly believable, details to fill in that picture. But these vivid details of our foresight are as fabricated and as convincing as our memories. What we leave out of these pictures is just as important as what we put in, but our hungry eye latches on to what it can see. Seeing is believing, after all, so we heavily underestimate the impact of what is not before us – maybe you forget to imagine the crowds of people, or the wasps or that faint smell of sewage – which is why when we turn up on holiday it so often does not meet our overly predefined expectations.

The second problem is presentism. Our imagination may take liberties by filling in the future with details that are overly vivid, but it is surprisingly unimaginative in terms of what it draws on for these details: namely the present. We stuff our versions of the future with what we know now and so conservatively disguise just how much changes over time. How we feel at the moment, for example, colours how we think we shall feel in future. Having eaten a wonderful Lebanese meal on Tuesday night it is almost impossible to imagine there and then (I can assert it, but not so easily imagine it) being the person who will eat three pizza slices too many on Friday night. This is because our imaginations draw on how we feel now to predict how we shall feel in most other situations. We know, intellectually, that time heals after a very painful break-up, say, but it is very hard to *imagine* feeling carefree.

The other side of presentism is that we don't adjust well for the passage of time. We treat it a bit like space. Unfortunately the fourth dimension has characteristics that do not always parallel the other three and this leads us into mistakes. If someone asks you to nominate local restaurants in which you might eat every night for a week it would make sense to choose a variety. We know familiarity breeds contempt and might choose seven different restaurants, so even if your favourite place is the local tandoori you might choose it only once. But if you were asked to choose a restaurant to go to once a month for the next seven months it is very easy to make the mistake of thinking variety is still the spice of life even when stretched over a longer term. We tend to underestimate the difference between the two cases. Seven months and seven days are much further apart than we can easily visualize. In the second case, it would make much more sense to stick with the India Palace every time, but the spatial metaphor telescopes down those months and makes it hard to recognize just how much time has passed in between.

The third problem is rationalization. We, just like Franklin, are good at reweaving our unruly experience into a coherent and positive (pan)gloss. A friend on a family holiday that constantly derailed from our original plan coined the word "idioptimism" to describe how willing we were to see everything working out for the best (in the best of all possible worlds). We have to be careful to be persuasive, of course. If our optimism, like Franklin's, is too idiotic we leave everyone staring in disbelief. Essentially we need to trigger the wilful suspension of disbelief in ourselves and others. We need our tales to be telling, and this is a more complex affair than our eye and brain striking a nice bargain between how the world is and how we would like it to be. We are always constructing and are therefore dependent on audiences to judge our constructions as we judge theirs. I shall return to this theme at the end of the chapter.

Essentially our proneness to "mis-wanting" comes from systematic distortions that arise out of our necessary attempts to predict how we shall feel in future, and explains why we are so often disappointed when our wishes are granted. Phillips refers to desire as a "queer form of prediction", and our future selves, like ungrateful children, can mock the efforts we make now for their own good. *What was I thinking when I moved to the country?* As Gilbert's research has shown:

> People very robustly want instant gratification right now, and want to be patient in the future. If you ask people, "Which do you want right now, fruit or chocolate?" they say, "Chocolate!" But if you ask, "Which one a week from now?" they will say, "Fruit." Now we want chocolate, cigarettes, and a trashy movie. In the future, we want to eat fruit, to quit smoking, and to watch Bergman films. (2006)

The self-protective illusions of foresight and insight (like the perceptual and cognitive illusions discussed in Chapter 1) are extraordinarily robust. For Eva the experience of having a child she did not love was a disappointing surprise on such a scale that it forced her into a level of self-scrutiny she had previously been able, like most of us, to avoid. She began to realize that her current perception of her future self was little more than a conventional set of assumptions about how people normally behave. After Kevin arrived she began to look beyond these assumptions:

> We have explicit expectations of ourselves in specific situations – beyond expectations, they are requirements ... Some of these are small: If we are given a surprise party, we will be delighted. Others are sizeable: If a parent dies, we will be grief-stricken. But perhaps in tandem with these expectations is the private fear that we will fail convention in the crunch.

That we will receive the fateful phone call and our mother is dead and we feel nothing. I wonder if this quiet unutterable little fear is even keener than the fear of the bad news itself: that we will discover ourselves to be monstrous ...

This kind of acknowledgement is more than most of us can bear. Most of us need to believe that our future selves are more predictable, trustworthy and reliable than that. Planning for the future – imagining alternatives, hoping and dreading – is one of the fundamental characteristics of being human, yet we do it surprisingly badly. If we cannot wish our wishes away we are left with explaining them away. We need to be skilful at describing our behaviour, motives and reasons in a way that travels between Franklin's near comical self-deception and the more ugly complexities that are clear to Kevin's shrewish eye. We become storytellers.

Telling tales

We need to be skilled storytellers to protect our reputations. "How eagerly we buy into each other's mythologies no matter how far fetched", says Eva in a letter to Franklin. Only by being placed in a position where she feels she has nothing to lose can she push past our "pat scripts" and voice those "unutterable little truths" that we routinely conceal, such as "how so much lying in a marriage is merely a matter of keeping quiet". And even then, feeling death in life, she needs to frame what happened, to choose whether to justify herself or to feel the weight of mortification. Her unanswered question is "Am I to blame for it all?", and she shifts between blaming herself, Kevin and Franklin. Her account of their tragic story cannot be unvarnished: there is no such thing. It is inevitably a creative work of reinvention, with the benefit of hindsight and has to take the form of a narrative. Our appetite for novels, films, stories from an early age testifies how deep this urge is in us. With our beginnings, middles and ends, we dream up a story about where we have come from and where we are going, in accordance with Kierkegaard's observation that life must be lived forwards but can only be understood backwards. Margaret Atwood vividly describes the difference between stories and experience:

> When you are in the middle of a story it isn't a story at all, but only a confusion; a dark roaring, a blindness, a wreckage of shattered glass and splintered wood; like a house in a whirlwind, or else a boat crushed by the icebergs or swept over the rapids, and all aboard powerless to stop it. It's only afterwards that it becomes anything like a story after all. When you are telling it, to yourself or to someone else.
>
> (Quoted in Tilley 2006: 65)

We sometimes, like the alcoholic Cheever or even the psychopathic Kevin, are required to answer the question "Why did I do that?", and struggle to do so when our motives appear to be thoroughly mixed. We apply retrospective justification on our action, not entirely because we want to conceal from ourselves, but because we can't tolerate meaninglessness. As described in Chapter 1 we strongly prefer the answer "because …" to "I don't know" even when it does little explanatory work. The psychoanalyst Leslie Farber comments that his trade is "backbreaking work … [since it is] constantly threatened by loss of meaning". He goes on to say that "almost any content no matter how debased or untrue, is more bearable than meaninglessness itself" (2000: 18); he might have added no matter how painful. Not knowing can be almost intolerable, as for the families of the "disappeared" in Pinochet's Chile, desperate to know the grim fate of their loved ones, or the audiences at the truth and reconciliation commission in South Africa, wanting to know exactly what happened, when, to whom, however harrowing it would be to hear. Ignorance may be bliss at times but we on the whole need a little knowledge, no matter how dangerous, even at the price of pain or distortion. And so we have developed automatic mechanisms for generating certainty: for allowing understanding, prediction and control even when these are unwarranted.

Why do we struggle, like Franklin, to accept our Janus-faced complexity? We see self-deception in others but not in the mirror, precisely because it works so well. Much as Eva can see Franklin's limits, she struggles to see her own. Eva comments to her husband that: "your ability to idealize would prove an awesome cudgel. There's no more doomed a struggle than a battle with the imaginary". One reason our accounts convince ourselves so effectively is that a good explanation simply "clicks into place", giving us a sense of relief. I see! Aha! Eureka! Gotcha! QED! In this the scientists who revel in the Keatsian connection between truth and beauty speak for us all. We gestaltist pattern-recognizers cling to whichever patterns we happen to see, until someone can replace it with something even more persuasive, or liberating.

But Farber teaches us to be suspicious of the aesthetic quality of such revelations. He remembers an episode when, undergoing analysis himself, he found he was surprisingly infuriated by the sound of a child practising the violin in the next room. He saw his overreaction as a clue to some unresolved conflict in himself, which led him to remember how he had disappointed his father by coming second in a violin competition he had entered as a child. This became the moment of crisis in his relationship with his over-ambitious father that changed everything between them: a "parting of the ways", he realized. But as Farber pondered on this account further he decided it was a seductive and self-deceptive dramatization of a far more humdrum reality. His father didn't care that much about the competition and their relationship did not go through a massive jolt at all. They in fact drifted apart much later. Farber was hooked on this account because:

revelation tends to have a certain loveliness of form that is quite unrelated to – and in fact may be quite in defiance of – what is revealed. "I see it now: I am a monster of self-absorption," may not seem especially self-congratulatory, but it is the sort of pronouncement that yields genuine satisfactions to its pronouncer, and these satisfactions are essentially aesthetic in character.

... Enthralled already by the ideology (psycho-analysis) that permitted – indeed provoked – these novelties of self-expression, and too naive – or too cowardly – to heed my tiny intimations of doubt about the authenticity of my behaviour, I played out the drama of my willed self-deception to the hilt. Self-deception but deliberate. Also known as lying.

(2000: 11)

These stories, while they hold up, give comfort in many ways; they reduce ambiguity, uncertainty and conflict (internal and external) and take some of the weight of responsibility for our behaviour off our shoulders. And they are harder to shrug off the neater they sound. Once we feel a satisfying click, "By Jove, I think I've got it", we sucker ourselves. The vividness of the exclamatory mode is no different in essence from the subtler ways we colour our more humdrum narratives. Our daily exaggerations and omissions have similarly deceptive qualities, as Eva came to recognize: "Funny how you dig yourself into a hole by the teaspoon – the smallest of compromises, the little roundings off or slight recastings of one emotion as another that is a tad nicer or more flattering". The Kevin in the back of her mind is sneering in cold recognition of these self-serving tics and weakens her self-belief. Eva may undermine Franklin's hopeful dreaming but in the same way Kevin undermines her own. Her version is more robust than Franklin's but is not strong enough to withstand the judgement of a sociopath. If Franklin and Kevin represent the extremes of hope and cynicism on either side, then Eva travelling between them helps us to reflect on how hard it is to be both honest and hopeful; in the ways she grapples with conflict, in how what she wants runs against what she believes she ought to want, she can help us to understand better how we can be our own worst enemies.

It is as though we have evolved both to want to believe and to being equally sceptical of those beliefs. The only way to pull off the trick of believing, given our deep doubts, is with cleverly (and often unconsciously) designed deceptions. It is a disorientating task to tug away at these implicit mechanisms of belief without giving way to endless cynicism and or uncertainty. A tolerance for ambiguity comes at a high price and can bring on a sense of vertigo. Yet I believe it is worth the effort for as we tell the more complex story we develop a stronger sense of the choices we have made. Along the way we arrive at a somewhat better understanding of what we want and have more hope of tackling our bad habits and compulsions.

But these insights do not come easily. Much of our thought and action is outside our conscious control. We have evolved to bury self-knowledge and have created cultures that reward self-deception and the consolations that come with it. So we need creative skills to articulate the nuances and half thoughts that subtly colour our normality. While storytelling can be a mechanism for covering up, it can also be a way to improve our self-knowledge. There are two kinds of what might be called "novelization": the kind we see in plot-driven airport blockbusters, which wrap us up into a simple story, with beginnings, middles and ends; and the other kind, such as *Kevin*, where we see an open-endedness, a susceptibility to the particular, that allows for the painful complexity of the human condition. We alternate between both, looking in turn through two ends of a telescope. I want to argue that we should, as much as we can bear, privilege the second kind of novelization over the first, and take things at face value as a last resort.

There will be no escape from scripts (pat or otherwise) in the end; that would be unbearable. As I've argued, here and in Chapter 1, we are believers at heart and need our narratives. It is just that we need our tales of ourselves to be more telling than Franklin's: if they are less "pat" they may stand up to scrutiny a little better; they may become more sustainable. There is, however, no guarantee of that, and along the way we have to face the fact that to jettison our scripts (always pat to some potent witness out there) can be more than we can bear; to take Eva's approach as far as we can is to risk ending up like Kevin. But being intelligible, credible, persuasive, ultimately likeable or loveable takes a great deal of skill. Not just the content of what we say and do but the way we say and do it is always in question. We must perform and manage impressions with alacrity. In doing so are we pulling the wool over each other's eyes? Or merely making a plea for what Coleridge called the "willing suspension of disbelief" in our audiences? I turn to these themes in the next chapter.

3. Deceiving each other: the techniques of sincerity

[To be natural] is such a very difficult pose to keep up.
(Oscar Wilde, *An Ideal Husband*)

At the start of the twentieth century the sociologist Charles Horton Cooley introduced the idea of the "looking-glass self" to suggest that people's identity, rather than internal to their psychology, is formed through a reflection of how they look from the outside. This self is no "mere mechanical reflection"; rather, it is populated by judging audiences whose imputed sentiments determine whether the reflection is flattering or not. There are three steps needed to create a looking-glass self: first you imagine how you appear in the eyes of an audience; next you imagine what they must be thinking of you; and finally you apply those imagined judgements to yourself. The process is nicely illustrated by this young internet blogger's description of her embarrassing moment:

> My debating tournament is over and I am eating at a beautiful restaurant, eating a wonderful fancy dinner of spaghetti. (No meatballs, I'm vegetarian.) Suddenly, I notice my boyfriend across the room and stand up quickly, knocking my plate of spaghetti all over my crisp white blouse and pressed black skirt.
> 1. I step outside of myself for a second. See a slenderish girl, wispy black hair, looking bewildered due to the not-quite-bloodlike stuff splattered all over her shirt.

2. Who does she think she is? Why is she dressed that fancily, anyway? Why does she act like she's all grown-up when obviously she can't even keep her spaghetti on her plate? Ugly. Oh, by the way, ugly hair too. How disgusting. I pity her.

3. I jolt back inside myself and feel my cheeks redden. Because now I am disgusted, imagining people looking upon me with pity.

On one level this is a commonplace observation. Who doubts that a sense of self is permeated by other people to some degree? We know others can hurt our feelings, or cheer us up, embarrass us, or redeem us with their love: we know we are social animals.

And yet an authentic self free of influence is an incredibly persistent illusion. We defiantly believe in an ideal of "true selves" persisting behind the masks of social convention. We feel that those who worry too much about the views of others lack integrity and know what the famously iconoclastic physicist Richard Feynman was getting at when he constantly reminded his wife Arlene, "What do you care what other people think?"

The ideal of the genuine, honest soul, free of the judgement of others, is as unrealistic as it is reassuring and requires that we bury the depth of our interdependence. So in our need for a flattering self-image we underestimate the quiet concealments that abound in adult life. People commit subtle acts of repair to their image, in passing, and then lose sight of them in the healing balm of forgetfulness. Think of secret consumptions (such as drinking from the carton, furtive lechery, binge eating), or the hidden machinery of our professional lives, such as mistakes covered up, or disguising the amount of effort (or the lack of it) that went into completing a task, or how couples conspiratorially conceal their "dirty laundry", or how naked bodies are hidden under uniforms and make-up, bent on marrying together an appearance and a manner. Only babies are unencumbered by these considerations. After all, wasn't Arlene Feynman only being required by Richard to care more about what *he* thought (of her independence) than "other people" – merely switching her audiences rather than abolishing them? Our "true selves" are "social selves" to the core.

Because looking-glass selves can never shake off their unreliable audiences we must resort to managing impressions so as to feel pride rather than shame. So to come across as "genuine" does not require adhering to the truth as such; rather, it means conjuring up a good performance that shows one as well-motivated and competent. To explore this rich terrain is to see how skilled and nimble people are at deceiving and persuading each other; how clever and self-contradictory they have come to be in pursuit of credibility. All this raises questions of sincerity and cynicism. What are we to make of the difference between honesty and fakery? Surely we can't function without that distinction. I shall start by exploring the complexities of truth-telling and the ambiguities of lying, before turning to judging audiences and the subtle techniques of persuasion.

Telling truths

Our jurisprudential ideal of a witness telling "the truth, the whole truth and nothing but the truth" is there to remind us of the obligation to meet our highest moral standards, and, I suppose, the fact that we need reminding indicates how rarely we meet them. Consider the British politician Jonathan Aitken's press conference to launch his libel suit in his hubristic progress to the witness stand:

> If it falls to me to start a fight to cut out the cancer of bent and twisted journalism in our country with the simple sword

of truth and the trusty shield of British fair play, so be it. I am ready for the fight – the fight against falsehood and those who peddle it. My fight begins today. Thank you and good afternoon.

Notwithstanding this florid announcement, Aitken was subsequently convicted for perjury. Clearly saying doesn't make it so, yet we idealize truth-telling and despise hypocrisy because we are believers at heart. *Homo credens* needs to sift the liars from the honest brokers in order to function effectively. Truth-telling, for all its fragility, is valued by society as a whole, and is the foundation of trust. We need to know what to believe and who to believe and so place great sanctions on bearers of false witness. Concomitantly we idealize the courage of those who "tell truth to power", especially if they risk great personal cost.

Michel Foucault's book *Fearless Speech* identifies *parrhesia* as one of the great virtues necessary to the flourishing of a healthy culture (his studies focus on ancient Greece and Rome):

> The one who uses *parrhesia* … is someone who says everything he has in his mind; he does not hide anything, but opens his heart and mind completely to other people …. and he does this by avoiding any kind of rhetorical form which would veil what he thinks. (2001: 12)

This version of truthfulness as authenticity never follows a multitude to do evil, and boldly declares its own biases and vested interests. And who would deny that *parrhesia* is our protection against the corruptions of power and vanity? We need our fearless speakers who, like the boy who saw through the emperor's new clothes, do not hide among the cowardly majority. It is easy to see how one can place this authentic, anti-hypocritical stance at the centre of one's moral world, and many have.

But what is it to tell the truth fearlessly? Truth is a notoriously complex topic in contemporary philosophy and, while every theoretical position is taken up by somebody, an innocent bystander might be surprised to gather how much agreement there is among scholars about what truth is not. First of all, as we saw in Chapter 1, we do not simply carve nature at its joints. Consider Bertrand Russell on this point in *An Inquiry into Meaning and Truth*:

> We all start from "naive realism", i.e. the doctrine that things are what they seem. We think that grass is green, that stones are hard, and snow is cold. But physics assures us the greenness of grass, the hardness of stones, and the coldness of snow, are not the greenness, hardness and coldness that we know in our experience, but something very different … Naive realism leads to physics, and physics, if true, shows that naive realism is false. (1940: 15)

In the irreverent and playful European (or continental) tradition of philosophy truth has long been under attack. The postmodern incredulity towards "grand narratives" has encouraged a subjective, socially constructed, relativistic picture that denies any foundation to the concept. This tradition has roots in Nietzsche, whose "perspectivism" denies the very idea of objective truth; he describes it in "On Truth and Lies in a Nonmoral Sense" as merely a "mobile army of metaphors, metonyms, and anthropomorphisms" and writes that those who have fooled themselves into pursuing it are only expressing a "will to power". A more domesticated version of this claim is found among neo-pragmatist philosophers, Richard Rorty being the most obvious example, for whom "is true" is merely the compliment people pay to sentences with which they agree. Rorty summarizes his own argument in *Contingency, Irony and Solidarity* like this: "since truth is a property of sentences, since sentences are dependent for their existence on vocabularies, and since vocabularies are made by human beings, so are truths" (1989: 21).

These relativistic-sounding claims (although Rorty claims not to be a relativist, but an "anti-representationalist" who admits causal links between words and the world) are emancipatory in spirit, in that they open up possibilities that are otherwise constrained by too narrow a focus on logic and evidence. Meanwhile the Anglo-Saxon, analytic philosophers typically shake their fists at this seemingly irresponsible self-indulgence. The main problem the analytical tradition has with the continental tradition is the latter's lack of respect for argument and evidence in supporting their claims. *Why Truth Matters* by Ophelia Benson and Jeremy Stangroom is a typical recent counterblast:

> Postmodern epistemic relativism itself relies heavily on rhetoric … and it enables rhetoric in others. So epistemic relativism makes possible a world where bad arguments and no evidence are helped to win public discussions over justified arguments and good evidence. This is emancipatory? Not in our view. It is not emancipatory because it helps emotive rhetoric to prevail over reason and evidence, which means it helps falsehood to prevail over truth. Being trapped in a world where lies can't be countered seems a strange idea of emancipation. (2006: 172)

Yet it is striking how analytic philosophers' own approaches to truth and meaning should make us wary of thinking there is great insight here to be found. The attempts to give truth some significant force, that is, a property that reliably separates warranted from unwarranted assertions, have been found wanting by many if not most philosophers of language. The coherence theory (that true statements are those that line up consistently with each other in a coherent web of beliefs), or the correspondence theory (that sentences pick out facts in the world) both founder when pressed. These more ambitious theories have been largely replaced in contemporary philosophy with various mechanisms for making truth relatively toothless. Donald Davidson, who is central to many of these debates, comments:

> We should not say that truth is correspondence, coherence, warranted assertability, ideally justified assertability, what is accepted in the conversation of the right people, what science will end up maintaining, what explains the convergence on single theories in science, or the success of our ordinary beliefs. To the extent that realism or antirealism depend on one or another of these views of truth we should refuse to endorse either. (1990: §309)

A controversial quietism is in the air. Today the debate among philosophers in the analytic tradition (admittedly to the disquiet of some, such as the quasi-realist Simon Blackburn) is dominated by slimmed down theories of "truth-lite", dubbed redundancy, disquotation, pragmatism or minimalism. These deflationary theories reduce the property of truth to a technical feature of semantics, which does little to guide us to the substantive truth in an everyday sense.

Yet, in everyday terms, the truth is often less contentious. We have an unshakeable "correspondence intuition" that won't be easily deflated. Common sense dictates that grass *is* green and stones *are* hard. When the stakes are low the truth seems unproblematic. As naive realists we can be coolly disinterested in our acceptance of uninteresting facts. But where facts become interesting they become clouded with our interests. At these times the truth is least available as an arbiter when we most need it; that is, when confronted with people who doubt the things we care about. So where we disagree – that Blair was right to support Bush, that reducing carbon emissions should be our top political priority, that the unborn foetus is a person, that smacking children is harmless, that history is the story of class struggle – the truth becomes hot property (its importance growing in line with its elusiveness). In these more interesting cases there is no consensus about the "truth of the matter", yet this is not to say we advocates become any less certain of the truth of our positions. There is nothing to stop both sides of an argument claiming *parrhesia*, leaving the little boy not knowing whose new clothes to point the finger at. Pro- and anti-abortion campaigners both think that they are telling the truth.

The point here is that all our machinery for persuasion, our techniques of sincerity only come into play when there is a difference of perspective at stake or a position to defend. People don't differ so much on the facts as on how they ought to be construed, and the language they choose to describe them is key to supporting those construals: "invasion" becomes "liberation"; "foetus" becomes "unborn child"; "redistributing wealth" becomes "confiscating earnings". People do not march to protest against the views of flat earthers, or use the arts of persuasion merely to claim that grass is green. But when the stakes are higher they begin to sound like Nietzsche's philosopher: a "wily spokesman for his own prejudices which he baptizes 'truths'" (1966: §5).

The whole truth and nothing but the truth?

There is another significant challenge to truth-telling that is expressed in the second part of the witness's oath. The very idea of telling the whole truth really is on a hiding to nothing. Think of the infinite range of irrelevant but true facts that taking this injunction seriously would require us to mention. "Yes, M'lud, I was driving too fast that night, and it was raining, and stones are hard, and grass is green and my Mother's maiden name is Conway …." This example may be absurd but it contains an important point. When we recount we have to select, and it is precisely at the boundaries of agreement that we can debate what we consider relevant to the story in question.

The whole truth is never what we are really asking for; we want the *relevant* facts and the question of what is relevant is not at all easily answered, and will be assessed inevitably by the beholder. The philosopher Paul Grice observed that "conversational implicatures", the meaning that lies between the lines, based on conventional maxims of what the speaker owes the hearer (relevance or brevity for instance), are what enables communication to happen effectively. The assumption of relevance in particular drives much of our judgement. If we go back to the example of Linda the feminist bank teller (see p. 15), we can see why so many people fail the test. The test bamboozles Gould, since he assumed, naturally enough, that Linda's political activism is *relevant* to the story, that is, providing information about the kind of bank teller she had turned out to be. Gould's homunculus, jumping up and down saying "She can't just be a bank teller – read the description", is making a point about not logic but the implicature in the description. The correct answer may be logical but it is not reasonable.

Specifying that we should stick to the relevant facts is easier said than done. The philosopher Jerry Fodor has argued that cutting out irrelevant facts is as necessary to reasoning as it is impossible to specify (to program a computer to do the job, for instance). That is to say, while we need to focus on the relevant information and ignore the rest there is no trusty algorithm that can tell you how to sift the apt wheat from the irrelevant chaff. This difficulty, first encountered by artificial intelligence programmers, is known as the frame problem after the cartoonists who, in creating the illusion of smooth movement, must decide which element of the image to change from frame to frame and which to leave unaltered. This kind of (abductive) reasoning, unlike deductive reasoning (which is a strictly logical derivation of conclusions from premises), is impossible to specify in the abstract. Only the audience can judge whether the relevant facts are in play. The judgement of my driving story, for instance, would differ if, in my list of facts, I suppressed the one about having been drinking whisky all evening, or selected the one about my mother (née Conway) being in need of emergency medical care. But there is no God's-eye view that can guarantee the relevance of the information I bring to bear. "I'm depraved on account of I'm deprived", says the defendant; "That's beside the point", says the prosecutor. Sure, we should stick to the *relevant* facts, but, whether we are defendants or prosecutors, relevance is precisely what is under scrutiny in any dispute.

More generally, since we are *choosing* what information to include in telling "the whole truth" we are judged on the skill with which we make those very choices. There is much at stake, for our reputations as nice and in control, in how the audience judges our grip on the whole truth; that is, our apparent perception of what is relevant to the account. If we have too tight a grip we omit key information and look like we're hiding something, while if we have too loose a grip we include too much and just sound crazy. This links into the two ways our credibility can fail: having a tight grip shows we are not nice, having a loose grip that we are not in control. This latter judgement, which doubts our competence, is as fatal to our reputation and trustworthiness as the former, which primarily doubts our motives.

The question of competence is equally threatened by the last part of the oath: "nothing but the truth". How would we sound if we spoke nothing but the truth? Foucault mentions that the Greeks condemned a form of bad *parrhesia*, what one might think of as incontinent truth-telling: "This pejorative sense occurs in Plato … as a characterization of the bad democratic constitution where everyone has the right to address his fellow citizens and to tell them anything – even the most stupid and dangerous things for the city" (2001: 13).

Where does that leave the little boy and the emperor? Who can tell the difference between good and bad *parrhesia*? It is the audience who must judge whether he was exhibiting fearless speech or was merely being "stupid and dangerous". What is typically at stake is whether the speaker is judged as believable in some broader sense by the audience. Whether in the case of Mr Collins arranging little compliments for Lady Catherine de Bourgh in *Pride and Prejudice* or Sacha Baron-Cohen's character Borat, who asks his dinner companion when he can have sex with her, we can agree that bad *parrhesia* is bad for credibility. The British tradition of the comedy of embarrassment from *Fawlty Towers* to *The Office* turns on just this point.

As discussed in Chapter 2, concealing mixed motives helps with a reputation for being nice and in control, which is required if one is to be creditable. And as we have seen, "too much information" from the speaker can make the audience incredulous. So the problem is that telling the truth convincingly relies on all the dramatic skills of telling a lie. One may feel that the idea of acting does not fit well with the idea of sincerity but, as W. H. Auden reminds us, "sincerity is technique". Truth will not out by itself. If it did we would not need courts and juries to attempt to sift out the innocent from the guilty. We would just believe the ones who weren't acting.

So the aim in narrating convincingly, it seems, is not to adhere to some literal concept of the Truth; rather, it is to earn a reputation for being credible. As will become clearer in this chapter, *Homo credens* is on the lookout not so much for abstract truth as for an understanding of motives and competence in our interlocutors. We are assessing how nice and in control we find each other, and tell appropriate tales to help improve our reflection in the looking glass that is other people.

This of course is not to deny the value of truth seeking activities such as science and the everyday demands that our claims are backed up by evidence and argument. But plausible storytelling and truth-telling have different logics; the second has a binary quality (true or false), while the first aspires to verisimilitude, a certain lifelikeness. And verisimilitude not literal truth is very often what we seek in each other. Logic can persuade but only a compelling story can seize someone's mind. To finish an argument with the rhetorical flourish "QED!" may convince your audience, but the way this is done successfully is rarely divorced from some sense of appropriateness. Appropriate content is largely about creating sympathetic weather. It is for this reason that rhetorical skills that create a compelling message can substitute nicely for argument. A punchline, for example, can bring debate to an end. When Ronald Reagan quipped, "I can't help noticing that everyone on the pro-abortion side of the argument has already been born", he managed to put his opponents on the back foot with wit rather than argument. Sometimes it's the way you tell 'em, and not what you say that counts.

So the truth, it seems, is rarely pure and never simple, as Oscar Wilde once quipped. Much as we may rhetorically brandish Aitken's "simple sword of truth", the mechanisms (whether in everyday life or a court of law) of being believable are clearly more complex than that. And there's a fine line between concocting a plausible sounding story and straying into falsehoods. In his essay "Lying on the Couch", Farber comments:

> In the pursuit of meaning in one's own life there is inevitably a temptation to estheticize ... as giving more deliberate and dramatic form to occasions and relations than they merited .... Everyone has, I imagine, experienced this temptation, and the difficulties it produces, in trying to present himself (to "tell it all") to a highly prized new friend. He swoops and sweeps across the past – and into the present – shaping, structuring, summarizing, condensing – lying, lying. That is not how it was; that is not who he is; not at all.   (2000: 11)

Economical truths and little white lies

Mark Twain is often attributed with the saying "A lie gets half way round the world before the truth can get its boots on". It probably goes further and faster now than ever before in human history. Our highly mediated culture means that the ubiquity and impact of public lies is greater than in previous times. For this reason our public figures are very closely scrutinized and can no longer hide under a veil of paternalist mystique. Listen to a news programme and note how much attention is given to who is pulling the wool over whose eyes. On the BBC's news analysis programme *Newsnight*, presenter Jeremy Paxman (whose professional mantra is said to be "Why is this lying bastard lying to me?") famously asked Michael Howard, then Home Secretary, the same question twelve times in a vain search for a straight answer.

It is still against the rules of etiquette in the House of Commons to call any Member of Parliament a liar, and anyone who does so will be censured by the Speaker. And yet, more subtle deceptions abound. We tend to think of spin as a recent political phenomenon but it has long been part of politics. Take this extract from a publication on the civil service published in 1941:

> the perfect reply to an embarrassing question in the House of Commons, is one that is brief, appears to answer the question completely, if challenged can be proved to be accurate in every word, gives no opening for awkward supplementaries, and discloses really nothing.   (Quoted in Giddings 1997: 87)

Nobody can be a leader, a hero, a carer, a pop star and an average guy or gal next door, with a blameless past, all at once. Yet this more and more is what a successful politician is expected to be, so dissembling becomes a necessity. As David Runciman observes (in his book *Political Hypocrisy*) the nature of politics requires that we are forced to choose between sincere conjurors and upright hypocrites and that the worst political hypocrisy comes from claiming one can have politics without hypocrisy. Yet to be caught in a barefaced lie could be death to a political reputation. The UK Secretary of State for War in the 1960s John Profumo was forced to resign after he admitted that he had lied to the House of Commons when he said there was "no impropriety whatsoever" in his relationship with Christine Keeler. But thanks to the conventions of everyday speech there are many ways to mislead without actually lying. President Clinton managed to avoid Profumo's fate when he announced to the American people that he "did not have sexual relations with that woman Monica Lewinsky". His technical definition of "sexual relations" (which did not encompass oral sex) enabled him to tell a misleading truth. Clinton's use of the word "is" in his now classic response to part of the post-Monica interrogation: "it depends what the meaning of 'is' is", received this response from his incredulous questioner: "I just want to make sure I understand you correctly. Do you mean to say that because you were not engaging in sexual activity with Miss Lewinsky during the deposition that the state-ment Mr Bennett made might be literally true?" Clinton replied:

> No sir, I mean at the time of the deposition that was well beyond any point of improper contact between me and Miss Lewinsky, so that anyone generally speaking in the present tense saying that that was not an improper relationship would be telling the truth. If that person said that there was not, in the present tense, the present tense encompassing many months. That is what I meant by that; I wasn't trying to give you a cute answer.　　　　　(Quoted in Pinker 2007: 205)

Steven Pinker contrasts this narrow adherence to the truth with George W. Bush's claim in his State of the Union address in January 2003 that "The British government has learned that Saddam Hussein recently sought significant quantities of uranium from Africa", and concluded that only Bush was technically lying (his use of the "factive" word "learned" crossed over that line) but that the key difference between them was only in the precision of their linguistic skill. Both statements were misleading but only Clinton managed to adhere to his goal which "was to be truthful, but not particularly helpful".

More generally politicians, bent on persuasion, are well aware of the biases and heuristics, described in Chapter 1, that help *Homo credens* leap to conclusions. Recency, vividness, framing, euphemism and many other arts of persuasion are pressed into service for all they are worth by any competent politician. They don't forget that Richard Nixon, it is said, lost the crucial televised debate with John F. Kennedy in 1960 because his five o'clock shadow made him look shifty. Step outside the political arena and similar conventions apply in all professional settings. Bare-faced lying may be beyond the pale, but with a covered face and a sidelong glance we are less timid. Obfuscation, omission, exaggeration, innuendo and deliberate ambiguity all provide ways of avoiding having to lie blatantly. We smile knowingly at estate agents' euphemisms, some of which are enumerated by Brian King in his book *The Lying Ape*. Here are the last few on his list with their translations:

- "Charming" means tiny
- "Compact" means tiny
- "Bijou" means tiny
- "Cosy" means divide Bijou by two
- "Studio" means … you can wash the dishes, watch the telly and answer the front door without getting up from the toilet.

(2006: 81)

But it is not just estate agents and politicians who play these games; we all do, of course. As the sociologist Erving Goffman says, "we find there is hardly a legitimate everyday vocation or relationship whose performers do not engage in concealed practices which are incompatible with fostered impressions" (1959: 71). We're back to Eva's "unutterable little truths". And Goffman echoes her insights:

> thus in well-adjusted marriages, we expect that each partner may keep from the other secrets having to do with financial matters, past experiences, current flirtations, indulgencies in "bad" or expensive habits, personal aspirations and worries, actions of children, true opinion held about relatives or mutual friends etc.
> (*Ibid.*)

Only some deceptions are unambiguously malign; the majority are more innocently motivated, such as loyalty to a friend, exaggeration to make a point, oversimplification in order to save time, or the courteous avoidance of embarrassment. We feign interest in someone else's hobby – "So when exactly does the grouse season start?"; delight when people arrive too early – "Oh look, you're here – wonderful!"; disappointment when they leave (a little too late) – "Must you go?"; pleasure on opening an ill-chosen present – "Gosh, I'm speechless!" We offer reasons for our behaviour that enable all concerned to save face. This is why it can be so embarrassing when you need to explain yourself in front of two people who differ in their relationship with you: your colleague and your client, or your father and your lover.

Pinker claims that the necessity of veiled speech is due to our extreme touchiness in negotiating changes in relationships. Politeness and tact help avoid the awkwardness of sounding bossy when asking a friend to pass the sugar. The same sensitivity occurs when making bribes, solicitations or threats. Indirect speech acts ("Come up and see my etchings") don't blurt out what is in mind but expect the listener to read between the lines, thus preserving plausible deniability on the part of the speaker (should the bribe, threat or seduction fail).

But, Pinker asks, if we all can read between these lines (etchings are not much of a euphemism after all), how could deniability on the part of the seducer be plausible. He argues that veiled language works because it trades on the distinction made by logicians between individual and mutual knowledge.

In *individual* knowledge:
A knows x
B knows x

In *mutual* knowledge
A knows x and B knows x
But B knows that A knows x, while A knows that B knows that A knows x, and so on.

Borat, in asking his dinner companion, "When can I have sex with you?", rather than mentioning etchings, created the *mutual* knowledge that made her unable to ignore his move. Had Borat used etchings to veil his attempt to change his relationship with his dinner companion from friendly to sexual, plausible deniability would have been possible. This is because he may know that etchings are an obvious come on and so may she (individual knowledge) yet she may not know for sure that he knows she knows that fact (i.e. maybe she was too naive to know that she was being seduced). By the same token he may not know that she knows he came on to her (maybe Borat was too dense). The lack of mutual knowledge means that they can maintain the fiction of friendship. Interestingly it is the relationship between direct speech and mutual knowledge that demonstrates the power of *parrhesia*. When the emperor walked in with his new clothes, each member of the audience could see he was wearing nothing. They had individual knowledge. But they didn't know that the others saw what they saw. Only when the boy shouted out did individual knowledge explode into mutual knowledge: each person in the audience then knew that the others couldn't see clothes either. This shows, more broadly, the importance of collectivities in helping reconstrue realities that are not convenient to the powerful. But collective action depends on mutual knowledge, so fearless speakers or whistleblowers help to stop dictators or organizations picking us off one at a time by creating it. At the same time these *parrhesiac* speakers need to be fearless since they take a risk that others do not think the same way.

If direct speech and *parrhesia* create mutual knowledge, then indirect speech and innuendo are important for avoiding it.

And haven't we all lied out of kindness? When a parent enthuses over their child's latest artistic production they are usually expressing love and affection through their "white" lie. Surely no question begs a diplomatic answer more than "Does my bum look big in this?" This kind of lying speaks to the moral injunction to avoid being cruel and is well invoked by poet Philip Larkin in "Talking in Bed" (1988), in which he remarks on the inability of even intimate couples to find words both true and kind or at least "not untrue and not unkind".

Another way of rendering Larkin's difficulty is to think of the contrast between being faithful to *our own* versions (being true) with being faithful to *other people's* versions (being kind) and in these terms one can see times when the moral pendulum ought to swing in the direction of serving others' needs first: better to be kind than true. Seamus Heaney's poem "Clearances" (1998) beautifully captures the subtle interplay of how fidelity to a relationship can mean less fidelity to oneself. The narrator tells how, in his relationship, his governing his tongue was a "genuinely well-adjusted adequate betrayal" of what he knew better, leaving the couple "allied and at bay".

We often govern our tongues in pursuit of something larger than our own self-interest, providing others with a more rose-tinted looking glass in which to view themselves. And who can deny Cooley's observation that "if we never tried to seem a little better than we are, how could we improve, 'or train ourselves, from the outside in'"? Not only can a lie be the kinder or nobler thing to do, it can on occasion be an ethical necessity. The Germans who hid Jews from the Gestapo during the Holocaust and misled them accordingly were acting heroically.

Yet, to talk up the benefits of "being economical with the truth" creates unease. And rightly so, for where does it end? In the same way that rationalizations such as "cruel to be kind" or "you have to break eggs to make an omelette" can justify harmful acts, protecting people from the truth "for their own sake" can be equally problematic. The problem with the notion of "virtuous" lies is that the person lied to has no say in assessing what it is deemed good for them not to know. Who says what a good lie is? Is it the philosopher Leo Strauss, who has been the intellectual inspiration for the neo-conservative movement in the United States? It is claimed that for Strauss, drawing on the idea of the Noble Lie in Plato's *Republic*, the truth is a luxury meant only for the elite few who can handle the dark and "sordid" reality behind the necessary illusions of the state. This justifies the right of the few to perpetrate the "Big Lie" over the many, *for their own good*. This picture of the secretive, duplicitous holders of power, masters of the universe, free of the expectations that bind the rest of humanity, is not a comfortable basis for the accumulation of political power.

The struggle over truth and lies that permeates our culture and behaviour means we need to be on the lookout. When the stakes are high, or unusual behaviour needs explaining, or mixed motives are in play, we cannot take the mere words people say for granted and must look to other cues to help assess their credibility. In short, we need to look for their motives.

On the set of the film *Marathon Man*, Dustin Hoffman is said to have gone to extreme lengths to get into role while preparing for the excruciating dental torture scene. He didn't sleep for three nights and worked himself up into a frenzy of anxiety while his co-star Laurence Olivier merely looked on from his chair. After a while Olivier turned to Hoffman, cigarette holder in hand, and languidly mused, "Why don't you try acting, dear boy ...". Hoffman, the method actor *par excellence*, wanted something deeper than that to create a truly convincing performance. He aspired to sincerity where his words and deeds matched his feelings.

When people debated whether Tony Blair was sincere or not they were judging his style, tone, delivery and passion as much as (if not more than) the content of what he said. The fact that emotions are hard to fake is invaluable as a mechanism for solving "commitment problems", as we saw in Chapter 1, but this, of course, provides all the more motivation for us to learn how to fake them. Legend has it that when Shirley Temple, the child actress, was asked by her director to cry on cue she responded by asking, "Which eye?" But Shirley is the exception that proves this rule. The difficulty in conjuring up an apt emotional response, even for skilled actors, leads film directors on occasion to duck the problem entirely. The audience has such an ear for the duff note that it is, on occasion, best to leave things unstated. In *Four Weddings and a Funeral* one character Gareth (played by Simon Callow) dies of a heart attack during a wedding party (which leads to the funeral of the title). When Charles (played by Hugh Grant) discovers the news of Gareth's death he has to tell his unknowing lover Matthew (John Hannah) of the devastating news across a raucous ceilidh and their exchange (from our viewpoint) is inaudible. We see no expression on the lover's face, across the crowded room, yet it was a deeply moving scene. A non-response is often the best response in extremis as it allows the viewer to inscribe their own imagined emotional reaction, and to plumb the depths of those still waters.

Who is to say what the right amount of emotion is? The outpouring of public emotion after the death of Diana, "the people's princess", was hotly debated afterwards. Was it a refreshingly open un-British response to a human tragedy or a mawkishly sentimental splash that did no one credit? Did Tony Blair's reading at her funeral switch you on or off? The trouble is that a good performance is always in the eye of the beholder. To be convincing requires the skills of an actor, and yet it is just the thought that someone might be acting that puts the audience on guard. We cannot function if we are not deemed trustworthy, nor if we are unable to trust others. So how does the sceptical witness ever come to trust a performer as she tiptoes through these tangled webs?

Unreliable audiences

[W]e work very hard to keep versions of ourselves in other people's minds; and, of course, the less appealing ones out of their minds. And yet everyone we meet invents us, whether we like it or not. Indeed nothing convinces us more of the existence of other people, of just how different they are from us, than what they can make of what we say to them. Our stories often become unrecognisable as they go from mouth to mouth ...   (Phillips 1996: 7)

Phillips perceptively reminds us how hard it is to seem as nice and in control as we would like. Our reputation depends on being perceived to be well motivated (or likeable or trustworthy) and basically competent (or skilful or sane), and people watching know that this is what we want to project and are assessing our behaviour closely. Sometimes we do this work in silence, using what Goffman calls "body gloss":

A girl in a university dormitory, desiring to receive mail although no one is in correspondence with her, may see that she is observed going to the dormitory mailbox, gives the appearance of looking for a particular piece of mail that she presumably has been expecting, and on finding that it isn't there yet shakes her head in puzzled wonderment – none of which she bothers to do when she thinks no one is observing her hopeless quest. (Quoted in Tilley 2006: 35)

Similarly when you arrive early at a restaurant and check your watch periodically you aren't just checking the time; you are sometimes conveying to the other diners that you are not alone. But silence is rarely enough; most of our messages are voiced, moving "from mouth to mouth", and are all the more risky for that. The philosopher Immanuel Levinas notes that:

Saying uncovers the one that speaks .... The unblocking of communication ..., is accomplished in saying .... It is in the risky uncovering of oneself, in sincerity, the breaking up of inwardness and the abandon of all shelter, exposure to traumas, vulnerability. (1998: 48–9)

The need to keep the "right versions" in other people's minds is both necessary and difficult for various reasons. The first challenge, as we have seen, is that an audience to any performance has an ear for the false note. Much of our conversation relies on what Goffman calls "the sweet guilt of conspirators", showing how careful we are not to tear down each others' polite face-saving facades. Think of the typical conversational dance, full of nods, turn-taking, repair work, asides, gambits, lapses in concentration (neatly covered up), invitations to agree, conflict avoidance, mutual reinforcement, awkward silences and assumptions of relevance. And yet, all along, we are breezily convinced we are just "being ourselves". When someone fails in their conspiratorial duty the results can be excruciating. According to legend, satirist Peter

Cook, at a literary soirée, once came across an old acquaintance he hadn't seen for years.

> Peter: Hello, John. Long time no see. What have you been up to lately?
> John: Oh, I'm writing a novel.
> Peter: [pause] Neither am I.

The fickle audience can be unforgiving. Even if a performance seems convincing, the audience reserves the right to change its mind when new evidence comes along to show the actor wasn't authorized to perform it. Quite often a competent performer is caught out for having the wrong credentials rather than for getting anything wrong. It is like legal advice from someone who it turns out only pretended to be trained: the advice is tainted even if absolutely correct. Paradoxically, the more accurate the fake the more we are threatened for, as Goffman points out, "a competent performance by someone who proves to be an impostor may weaken in our minds the moral connection between legitimate authorization to play a part and the capacity to play it" (1959: 66–7). But the connection is not just moral; the very nature of a competent performance requires a background belief that the performer is qualified both in expertise and intent. A sonnet reads differently if we discover it was randomly generated by a computer or a million typing monkeys than if it had come from a "real poet".

This leads on to the next area of difficulty. While the fake lawyer is easily seen as unqualified for the role, the qualifications of a "real poet" are rather more elusive. If we return to Peter Cook's interlocutor, what does John's claim "I'm writing a novel" imply, in fact, about his credentials? What is it to be a *bona fide* novelist anyway? Is it enough to be dabbling in a writing hobby with no hope of being published? Many roles we adopt have unspecifiable credentials. Unlike pretending to be a lawyer or doctor, there are no letters after the name of someone claiming to be a music lover. I once overheard a comment from a friend accepting the credentials of one such claim because "he had said he loved Brahms", the implication being that this was a less clichéd, and thus more credible/creditable, response than liking Mozart or Beethoven.

Our assessment of whether someone is hiding something depends on our perception of what he or she has to gain from our believing their story. If we spot a self-serving motive we switch on the sceptical antennae. The motive in question, as for Peter Cook's interlocutor, is usually an attempt to boost status. The "excess statements" of those few who do not fear being stigmatized is further evidence of their fearlessness and so boosts that status further. These shameless performances subtly reinforce status rather than trying to hide it or improve it. It is for this kind of reason that convincing performances can come from what the sociologist Thorstein Veblen called "conspicuous consumption". Billionaires can reduce their peccadilloes to mere eccentricities, and spend money for no reason other than to prove that they have so much of it. Apparently the bar stools on Aristotle Onassis's yacht *Christina* are covered with the super soft, and shatteringly expensive, foreskin of the sperm whale penis. As F. Scott Fitzgerald once remarked, the rich "are different from you and me". Film stars and billionaires literally, and thus metaphorically, have more credit. The same goes for other signs of being part of society's elite, such as enormous power or beauty.

This may be why the slightest chink in their armour creates a tabloid feeding frenzy, avidly consumed by a public with an appetite for rough justice. As Goffman notes, "if we grudgingly allow certain symbols of status to establish a performer's right to a given treatment, we are always ready to pounce on chinks in his symbolic armour in order to discredit his pretensions" (1959: 66). One of the iconically "discrediting" images in British politics is 1980s' footage of then Labour Party leader Neil Kinnock and his wife

Glenys struggling to escape the surf coming in on Brighton beach; as they scrambled away from the wave they fell over each other into the water. Some say an election slipped away in that partic-ular moment. As discussed in Chapter 1 we are psychologically prone to believing that a picture tells a thousand words, but the significance of any picture is contextualized by how we interpret the motives in play. Was it mean to mock the Kinnocks who were innocently responding to the laws of gravity? Or did we see them as trying to manipulate us with their breezy, carefree beach scene, a mere charisma-pumping photo op that went gratifyingly wrong? Kinnock had even quipped at the time that he could walk on water! If we think we are watching a performance, we pounce on those chinks.

Status and the anxieties that come from gaining or losing it are some of the key drivers of how we assess each others' claims. We detect and punish cheats with a skill and alacrity that befits the social animal we have evolved to be, as explored in Chapter 1. The scale of the self-interest in play provides the context in which we can measure the betrayal that comes from managing impres-sions, and the punishment that follows when unveiled. Had John used the less aggrandizing but still euphemistic "I'm in between jobs" in answer to the question, Peter Cook would have had less reason to pounce. If the person we encounter has nothing to gain over us but is only trying to save their performance from complete collapse we can be gracious. John's line "I'm writing a novel" may not have been so venal an attempt to raise his status above Peter Cook's. Maybe it was an act of desperation: the maladroit lunge of someone so stigmatized he felt too ashamed to think straight in the presence of such a superior and frightening audience. In this case Cook's retort might be judged intolerably cruel. We are constantly judging according to an assessment of the motives in play, and the motives of the desperate are not hubristic or hypocritical; they are just trying to get by.

Even when we get it all right we cannot rely on our audience judging us kindly. So we play safe. People tend to avoid situations in which they might lose face; and they cooperate, "finding there is much to be gained from venturing nothing", as Goffman said (quoted in Lemert & Branaman 1997: 110). When playing safe is not an option you need to act, and in so doing you put yourself in the hands of the audience. Whether we, as audiences, judge you harshly or cut you some slack depends a great deal on the kinds of interests we see you as serving.

The shameful limits of deception

Despite skilled efforts to manage impressions of us in our audiences, we will never be fully sure to succeed. People leak the cues they wish to conceal, however good their acting skills. Their audiences are, after all, equally skilled in these techniques, and it takes one to know one. Much of the motive for deception is the avoidance of embarrassment or worse, humiliation and shame:

> [I]n an important sense there is only one complete unblushing male in America: a young, married, white, urban, northern, heterosexual Protestant father of college education, fully employed, of good complexion, weight, and height, and a recent record in sports .... Any male who fails to qualify in any of these ways is likely to view himself – during moments at least – as unworthy, incomplete, and inferior.
>
> (Goffman 1963: 128)

Unlike guilt, which spurs us to make reparations or apologise, shame makes us want to disappear. To be stigmatized is to be exposed when we are not ready for it and have nowhere to hide. We like to be covered up while being able to see, peeking through our fingers, but often we are not quick enough and get stuck in the glare, like Adam after the fall, who could do nothing but turn in on himself and cover his face. In order to avoid losing face we need to keep a separation from the front-stage performances we have been describing and a backstage region where we can hide from view, prepare for exposure and keep our diverse audiences away from each other.

The threat of a painful gaffe puts reputations on the line in every social encounter. Trivial mishaps such as spilling a plate of spaghetti into your lap, tripping up while dancing, wearing the wrong clothes for the occasion or calling a colleague by the wrong name can haunt for a long time. In fact the stigmatized and ashamed have such low expectations of pulling off an adequate performance they can be persuaded or seduced into believing they are fakes (as can anyone prone to self-doubt). The seduction works because the seduced sometimes wants to match the judgement of the superior even if that judgement is shattering. They collaborate. In a striking metaphor Richard Sennett describes the superior as:

> like a guard standing at a border crossing, simultaneously beckoning to others while refusing to accept their passports as valid. They insist, he then says "let me show you what a valid passport looks like." Now they are hooked: "but my passport looks just like that!" The seduction is about to occur; the guard ruefully demurs, "well, it looks the same, but I'm not sure." And then is consummated: the immigrant looks at his documents and ruefully reflects, "my passport, although genuine, was not good enough." (2003: 91)

There is an intrinsic challenge to our ability to manipulate the judgement of others. This is to do with the fact that other people's moral and aesthetic judgements of us are uncomfortably inter-linked. Conventionally speaking we tend to the view that it is only

89

fair to judge someone ill or well for things they can control. We, like Martin Luther King, want our children to be judged not "by the colour of their skin but by the content of their character". But this poignant dream is an illusory one. We are reminded of the brutal fact of aesthetic judgements on us when we are ashamed of things that are not our fault and humiliated despite our good intentions: despite our efforts to secure a good reputation.

It turns out that moral and aesthetic virtues are readily convertible currency. The cruel fact is that the aesthetic component is just as valuable to us as the moral even though, conventionally speaking, we have less control over it. This is why Winston Churchill could put down Lady Astor with the famous retort to her accusation "Winston, you're drunk!": "Yes, Madam, but you are ugly, and in the morning I shall be sober". The moral flaw of being drunk is here traded in for the aesthetic one of being ugly. We judge people both aesthetically *and* morally and this is a difficult thing to accept. Who do we invite for dinner? People we admire for their moral worth or those we relish for their entertainment value? Either of these two dimensions can be in play. If I judge someone negatively for overeating it could be to see them as morally flawed, and blame them for being greedy and selfish, or aesthetically flawed because I am simply repelled by the sight of their gobbling.

This is why we are so often drawn to people who are bad for us ("you are awful, but I like you"). In fact, one can often expect to be judged well, aesthetically, by admitting to moral failings. When we berate ourselves for drinking too much we somehow manage to convey that we have exciting social lives. We adorn ourselves and each other with morally dubious labels to enhance our aesthetic attributes, and recognize that many people in this world are, like Rushdie's cream cakes, "naughty but nice". Think of men ruefully recounting their sexual encounters while proving subtly that they are "real men", or those who admit their hot headedness (always getting into trouble) to flaunt their strength. A misspent youth turns out to have been a good investment.

Both aesthetic and moral judgements it seems are about *worth*: "cred", the interchangeable currency of *Homo credens*. The two dimensions that we and Martin Luther King would like to keep separate are thus constantly blurred, and so by conveying that a failing is merely aesthetic and not a moral flaw we do not thereby escape the harsh judgement of others; we are only trading denouncement for repulsion. The same goes for our more positive judgements. Take integrity. Somebody is seen as having integrity in two ways. The first is that they can be counted on to keep their promises, or resist temptation. The second is that their life has a kind of harmony. They have such a quality of soul that they would not be tempted in the first place. This great-souled quality is something to admire, like a painting, even if not necessarily something that was earned.

If, as it seems, we can be judged equally for characteristics whether we have control over them or not there is no reliable escape from the threat of shame. Yet this does not stop us casting around for ways to duck the judgement that we are not nice. We have devised innumerable ways to place our agency out of reach, and our choices out of our hands, because convention enables the belief that what is outside of our control is not our fault. Or does it? Chapter 4 explores the limits of this consolation and the moral consequences that flow from accepting the moral choices we do not like to admit we have made.

4. "It's beyond my control" and other moral masquerades

> Only the descent into the hell of self-knowledge can pave the
> way to godliness.   (Immanuel Kant,
> *Groundwork of the Metaphysics of Morals*)

In the film *Dangerous Liaisons* the Vicomte De Valmont (played
by John Malkovich) breaks up with Madame De Tourvel (Michelle
Pfeiffer), sinking her into a spiral of grief that leads to her death,
and ultimately his own too. He loves her deeply but is required to
split up with her by his pride, which will not have him submit to
love. During the brutal conversation she begs him to reconsider and
asks, "Do you want to kill me?", to which he replies, "You have given
me great pleasure but I simply cannot bring myself to regret leaving
you. It's the way of the world. Quite *beyond my control.*" Sound
familiar? In the fable of the scorpion and the frog that opened the
Introduction, the only explanation for the scorpion's destructive
(and self-destructive) act put it beyond his control with the line
"It's in my nature". We often play Valmont's scorpion to Madame de
Tourvel's frog, using phrases such as "it's not my fault, I can't help
it", "mistakes were made (but not by me)", "boys will be boys" and
"*que sera sera*" all harnessed in an effort to feel less accountable for
one's actions. David Brent in the British comedy *The Office* said it
best when explaining to his team that some of them would be losing
their jobs: "It's out of my hands, and even if it were in my hands, my
hands are tied" (Gervais & Merchant 2003). *Others* may only have

themselves to blame, but *we* have many other candidates, a wide array of external or internal forces conveniently invoked to reduce the weight of agency: "the rules", parents, bad luck, gods, star signs, genes, common sense, personality, make up, tradition, chemistry or culture, all representing the gusts of fate on which we appear to be helplessly buffeted. Of all the deceptions to which we are prone, the moral dodge of exculpation, the one that makes us seem more creditable and less blameworthy, is perhaps the most profound.

Contrary to his helpless-sounding rhetoric, Valmont fashioned the scorpion-like mantra quite deliberately to get himself through a difficult emotional task. It was a psychological trick of the light, conjured up by a rival lover in the background, which temporarily disguised the cruel choice he was making and placed it out of his reach. In contrast with the automaticity of a scorpion following its ineluctable drives, Valmont was working *hard*; in fact he was stricken by the task of breaking up with his lover and had to repeat the refrain eight times in order to complete the separation. As I have argued, *Homo credens* normally likes to appear nice *and* in control, but on occasion, especially when faced with the moral weight of a cruel, cowardly or selfish act to face up to, the only hope of retaining a shred of niceness is to give up that sense of control. Like Jean-Paul Sartre's fictional character Antoine Roquentin in *Nausea* we can find our freedom to be a nauseating burden.

But what if there is a grain of truth in Valmont's self-exculpation? After all, our excuses would have little rhetorical weight if they didn't sound plausible. And clearly there are many aspects of our lives that are indeed beyond our control. I can't choose my parents, the colour of my skin or the place of my birth. Earlier chapters explored areas over which we have little control: our unconscious proneness to distorting illusions, our emotional responses and unruly desires, the cultural climates in which we breathe. In this chapter some of these will be revisited to see their implications for our ethics. To explore how well people can free themselves from the limits on their actions requires that we explore those limits first: limits that operate on levels that vary from the physiological to the cultural and are not to be taken lightly. These constraints on our behaviour all close down the sense of agency that is essential for moral responsibility. The closer we look at them, the more things start to look beyond our control after all.

And yet our sense of freedom, despite these constraints, seems to persist. It is hard to imagine a human culture in which there is no place for praise or blame, for striving or regretting. Many moral philosophers argue that we have genuine choices and therefore can be held to account for them; without choices there can be no morality. In their appeal to our more responsible natures we are urged to override short-term impulses and herd mentality. Instead they invite us to follow universal and impartial moral principles, such as the golden rule, and thereby leave self-serving prejudices at the door. Kant's *categorical imperative*, which places the emphasis on moral duty rather than inclination or consequences, for instance, never condones a lie (however well intentioned), while the "consequentialist" claim that the end justifies the means of utilitarians such as Jeremy Bentham and John Stuart Mill leads us to put our gut feelings to one side and focus on what brings the greatest happiness to the greatest number. These abstract mechanisms are offered to help us override our human frailties and churn out impartially valid moral judgements.

Yet if we do have choices we must face the fact that our moral standards are pretty low. To judge from the ubiquity of moral hypocrisy in our daily lives (Valmont is hardly an exception) we may feel condemned to accept Hamlet's sober judgement: "Use every man after his desert, and who should 'scape whipping?" On this view, everyone deserves to be punished. We are often forced into a more humble acknowledgement that the high-minded injunctions of moral philosophy are up against profound challenges. As E. O. Wilson the entomologist once said of Marxism, nice idea, wrong species. Even Kant had his pessimistic moments:

We like to flatter ourselves by falsely taking credit for a more
noble motive .... A cool observer, one that does not mistake
the wish for the good, however lively, for its reality, may sometimes doubt whether true virtue is actually found anywhere in
the world ...   (Quoted in Batson 2008: 52)

And so in our efforts to escape whipping, we cook the facts. Self-
exculpation, of course, tends to happen when things go badly. We
overstate our helplessness as Valmont did when things get sticky,
but we also take unwarranted credit when things go well. We have a
strong self-serving tendency to use whichever view is more convenient. With matters of regret, such as a relationship failing, it's easier
to claim that "we drifted apart" than to acknowledge the quiet decisions that were made along the way that led to this end. On the
other hand where things have turned out well (a good career or
happy, successful children), we are much more likely to take the
credit, and understate the amount of good fortune in play, although
modesty forbids crowing too loudly.

This chapter is primarily concerned with moral accountability
for our choices and the constraints that alleviate this pressure: how
our cowardly, greedy, mean-minded actions, when caught in the
light, trigger us to look for excuses, while, by the same token, we
take uneasy credit for lucky accidents that make us look brave,
clever and kind. But to set the discussion in a more vivid context
we can start with a relevant example or two.

Lord Jim's choice

There is an increasingly fashionable pessimism about the scope and
range of true choices and motives. It is well expressed by the philosopher John Gray who, in his uncompromising book *Straw Dogs*,
claims "humans think they are free, conscious beings, but in truth

they are deluded animals" (2002: 120). After Darwin, says Gray, we should know better than to cling to the self-aggrandizing daydream that people are above other animals. This "secular religion" of free will and true choices offers cruel and misleading hope and denies our fundamentally animal natures. Our self-image needs to be deflated.

Gray cites Joseph Conrad's novel *Lord Jim* to make his point. Jim, the first mate aboard the *Patna*, dreams youthful dreams of heroism and of the daring act that will prove his courage, only to fail the test when it comes. En route to Mecca the *Patna*'s hull hits a submerged object and the ship starts to sink, along with its human cargo of eight hundred Muslims making their pilgrimage. Jim simply watches as the captain and crew abandon ship, a mere spectator, and then finds himself, as if by magic, also in the lifeboat:

"I had jumped." He checked himself, averted his gaze ...
"It seems," he added.

He "averted his gaze" and "it seems" saved himself. Even though the *Patna* survives, as do all the pilgrims, who are towed safely to harbour, Jim's self-respect does not. He faces the disgrace of a public enquiry and is haunted privately by a gnawing fear that he is a coward. He will never, as we say, be the same. Yet, for Gray this is too much responsibility to take on. It is more than he should have to bear because Gray believes (and draws on neuroscientific research to support the claim) that we cannot "be authors of our own acts". We are more like the scorpion than we like to think because "we are descendants of a long lineage only a fraction of which is human. We are far more than the traces other humans have left in us" (2002: 79). These ancient encryptions shape our options and destiny far more than our self-image normally allows.

This thought is tempting when things go badly because, like the scorpion, we prefer not to take the full weight of painful events.

Of course we want the answer to the question "Am I to blame?" to be "No, it's not your fault". Yet Jim resists this temptation (if it ever occurred to him). He is baffled by his action but, unlike Valmont, will not absolve himself of the responsibility. He never recovers because he is stuck in the "incessant oscillation between the perspective of an actor and that of a spectator" (*ibid.*: 67); that is to say he can't believe what he did, but he can't deny that he did it. He should, in Gray's view, let himself off this twin-pronged hook and realize that it was his destiny to jump and it is foolish to believe he could have avoided this tragic fate. Instead Jim feels guilty as charged, and, desperate to start afresh with a clean slate, he spends the rest of his life in a vain search for redemption: a reason to judge himself well. Gray hands the last word to Marlowe, the narrator of Lord Jim's tribulations: "And I felt sad. A clean slate, did he say? As if the initial word of each our destiny were not graven in imperishable characters on the face of a rock" (*ibid.*: 69, quoting Conrad).

Do we need to feel as sad as Gray or Marlowe? Sometimes we do. There is necessary consolation in accepting the sad facts of destiny, when the alternative is the excruciating thought that we are to blame. Sometimes moral accountability can be too much to ask for. Sophie's choice, in the book and film of that name, which was to choose at gunpoint which of her two children to save, was surely anything but a meaningful one. While Sophie could never shirk the guilt that came from this horrific dilemma, and eventually committed suicide, anyone looking on at her atrocious predicament would surely sympathize with whatever mechanism she might have used to lift the unbearable weight. Perhaps Lord Jim should have succumbed to his tragic fate and recognized that he didn't in fact "jump"; rather, he was "pushed" by events. We can sympathize with Jim's plight ("there but for fortune go I") and should be leery of rushing to judgement unless we have passed that test ourselves.

Unfortunately the denial of the possibility of cowardice can equally apply to the possibility of heroism too. Had Jim not jumped, but instead rushed to help the pilgrims, presumably Gray would not have seen reason to give him credit either: and maybe with good reason. Bravery and cowardice are beside the point if there is nothing one could have done differently. Isn't it true that we bandy the word "brave" about more loosely than we should? We call sufferers of disabilities or dangerous illnesses "brave" just in virtue of the difficulties they face, rather than their reactions to their predicament. In resisting this sentimentality the journalist John Diamond, who chronicled his ultimately unsuccessful battle with throat cancer, echoed Gray's uncompromising stance and denied any bravery on his part. Diamond's unflinchingly clear-eyed view was that any response to such a grave situation is legitimate, neither brave nor cowardly, whether you curl up in the corner and cry or, like him, broadcast the consultant telling you his diagnosis on national television.

But how far can we go in putting aside our capacity to praise or blame? Take another decision that can stand as the counterpoint to Lord Jim's. In late October 2005, just before Diwali, the Hindu Festival of Lights, Kuldeep Singh stopped his crowded bus on a busy street in Delhi to investigate the commotion in the back. Passengers told him that a man in his early twenties had left a bag on his seat with wires hanging out. Kuldeep was certain it was a bomb. He grabbed the bag and jumped off the bus just in time, but the bomb detonated as he tried to throw it away. He was blinded in one eye and lost two fingers off his right hand in the blast but he saved the lives of his passengers. Two other bombs went off in Delhi that day, killing over sixty people.

Reports of Singh's extraordinary act congratulated him on the one hand for acting "without thinking", and on the other for having "great presence of mind". Well, which was it? Reports say he acted "automatically" *and* that he decided "what was best to do in the circumstances". Did he think of his heavily pregnant wife, or the fact that the bus was powered by eight highly explosive canisters of compressed natural gas? Furthermore, can he be a hero if, as his friends suggest, he is a man who "knows no fear"? Heroism surely implies conquering fear, not fearlessness. Was it "in his nature" to act so bravely, or did he make a difficult moral choice? Can even he tell us why he did it? Can he trust his own version of events? Will he ever regret what he did? Would you, or Lord Jim, have done the same?

To answer the question "Why did I do that?" is surprisingly difficult. On this point Simon Blackburn is fond of quoting Queen Elizabeth II at the time of Princess Diana's death, amid the surrounding atmosphere of intrigue: "There are dark forces at work, of which we know nothing". I shall explore some features of these dark forces, two views in particular: the internal pressures that come from emotion, and the external pressures exerted by other people and bad luck. After exploring these grounds for pessimism we shall be better placed to look at the question of free will and accountability more directly.

Gut reactions

There are two ways that emotions can represent the dark forces that constrain the making of free moral choices. The first is to do with their involuntary nature, and the second is to do with how entangled they are with a capacity for moral judgement.

As we saw in earlier chapters, the emotions evolved as a way to reinforce trustworthiness precisely by being beyond our control to some degree. If we, like Shirley Temple, can cry on demand (even to the point of asking "Which eye?"), then there's no way of separating the genuine from the bogus performer. So, the argument goes, emotions evolved to be hard to control and therefore hard to fake in order to work as stamps of credibility. Accordingly, if we are genuinely overcome by rage or love or panic (think of the fatalistic consequences of Othello's jealousy) how is it possible to think we can alter our course of action? We routinely let people off the hook because they are overcome by an emotion that stops them making the right choice, and this common-sense judgement is to varying degrees enshrined in legal defences on grounds of diminished responsibility or temporary insanity.

This brings us to the second way emotion can constrain ethics. The human moral sense is deeply rooted in emotional reflexes. It is easy to see why this thought is uncomfortable. Moral judgement surely means making choices based on more independent principles than how one merely feels. We talk, at our best, as if principles of right and wrong are, or at least should be, free of the taint of unruly passions. But this is misleading rhetoric. Disgust, empathy, fear, anger, guilt, shame and so on all shape and constitute our ability to make moral choices rather more than we usually admit. Far from being Kantian rational moral agents acting in accordance with abstract principles, we are social animals mired in meat and crooked timber.

One way to see the link between emotion and morality is the "runaway trolley" example dreamed up by the philosopher Philippa Foot. In this thought experiment a train trolley has come loose and is careering down the tracks on its way to smash into five railway workers who cannot see the danger and will certainly be killed. You happen to be standing by a lever that if pulled will shift the trolley into a siding, except that there is a lone worker in the siding who will be killed if you do so. The question is should you pull the lever and save the five lives in exchange for one? In the second version of the story you are on a bridge watching the runaway trolley, and the only thing you can do to stop it is push a large man who happens to be leaning over the side, into its path. Again should you do it? Most people in answering this question find they say yes to the first version and no to the second, even though they both involve the exchange of one life for five. This result has been tested by the psychologist Marc Hauser in surveys of over 150,000 people, 90 per cent of whom follow the pattern: yes to pulling the lever, no to pushing the man. Our gut feeling, not our rational assessment, makes the second choice wrong. I say "gut feeling" but neuroscientists have identified the emotional response as residing in a part of the brain called the ventromedial prefrontal cortex (vmPFC). People with damaged vmPFCs push that large man just as easily as pulling the lever. Similarly, those of us with intact vmPFCs, would not allow doctors to pounce on a healthy person to harvest their organs to save the lives of five patients who would die without them. Our emotional response predominates over any abstract rational calculation as to what is the right thing to do.

An emotional basis to morality can be unsettling. One might worry that inconsistent reasoning can lead to bad decisions and moral hypocrisy. Think of, for instance, the plausible sounding argument that it is wrong to eat meat if you are not able to kill the animal from which it came. But without the right emotional responses to guide these judgements, surely our morality swings free of something important. Are we not right to resist pushing the large man over the bridge even if the consequences seem to justify doing so? Someone who can push the man over as easily as pull a lever has a core part of their moral machinery missing, an emotional blind spot, and could presumably commit cruelty without compunction. In short, contrary to the view that our feelings should be irrelevant to our morality, we need our emotional repertoire if we are to be moral agents. By underpinning many of our moral responses, and by being outside our rational control our emotions lead us to trust ourselves, in the same way they help other people to trust us. Haven't you been to a funeral or a wedding and almost felt relief that genuine emotions were welling up in you, rather than feeling nothing and having merely to act appropriately?

Our emotions are a core part of our moral sense but they also misfire, and lead moral judgements astray. For example, we experience disgust, which presumably evolved to protect us from disease, even when there is no reason to. Dunk a sterilized cockroach, or a piece of plastic shaped like faeces, into a glass of water and people refuse to drink it. The knowledge that the water is fine does little to inhibit the reaction of disgust. We are in hock to the "contagion principle", which implies that when two things make contact some of their properties transfer in a process of what anthropologists call "sympathetic magic": in this case the gut feeling that says "you are what you eat". Disgusting things look immoral, and immoral things look disgusting, and this blend is woven into our consciousness to a profound degree. As the psychologist Paul Rozin's work on disgust suggests, there is a potent link between aggression and the inability to tolerate this aspect of our animal nature. The revulsion of racists and homophobes towards the groups they oppress has this emotional tone (as can the contempt and repulsion felt in return by those of us who oppose them). Rozin comments that "disgust evolves culturally, and develops from a system to protect the *body* from harm to a system to protect the *soul* from harm" (Penn Society of Arts and Sciences 1997). This moralization process leads us, as explored at the end of Chapter 3, to blend the moral and the aesthetic, in defiance of Martin Luther King's laudable dream.

Fear is similarly disconnected from what it was originally designed to do, that is, protect us from danger. Snakes cause more fear than cars, spiders more than electric sockets, even though the thing people fear more is far less dangerous in each case. Again, a link between our ethics and emotional responses, while necessary, can leave us with alarming consequences for our moral choices. How often do governments create a climate of fear to garner the population's support for curbing their own liberties, or to victimize minorities? Fear makes a bad advisor.

Not only do our emotional and therefore moral reactions happen to some extent involuntarily, but these tendencies can be easily manipulated. Tearjerking films can make you cry while remaining aware of the conjured-up emptiness of the emotion. Sales techniques trade on our sense of fairness by offering discounts or a give away so as to prompt you to give something back in return. A picture is worth a thousand words, because it summons up our emotions. It is widely agreed that Nick Ut's Pulitzer prize-winning picture of Kim Phúc, a nine-year-old girl running naked and burned after a Napalm attack, transformed public sentiment about the Vietnam War. And knowing the power of the image, politicians persuade us of their sincerity and decency in photo ops: they kiss babies or feed hamburgers to their children during the BSE crisis (with, for good or ill, vivid consequences for their reputations). Research tells us that good-looking people are seen as morally good, and that tall people are more likely to run companies. These reflexes are nicely blended in the "Warren Harding" effect. Warren Harding is widely acknowledged to have been the worst US president in history (although the record books are always being updated!). When people were asked why they voted for this tall, pleasant and handsome but intellectually unqualified candidate they could only answer that he just "looked presidential". It can seem sometimes that our emotional strings are just waiting for the right puppeteer to come along and pull them.

So gut feeling is a core part of our moral capacity and at the same time threatens our ability to act morally. What might this mean for our judgement of Jim, Singh and Diamond? In *The Mystery of Courage*, professor of law William Ian Miller explores examples of apparent bravery to assess whether there is an "agreed-upon inner state" that drives heroic action and concludes that there is not:

Sometimes people just blank: "It had to be done, somebody yelled 'Medic!' I ran to help the guy." Most of the time, though, they're just confused. There's too much noise. There are no thoughts at all. They're engaged in automatic behaviors. For others, the internal state was simply terror, fear – the exact same internal state that the coward has. So many of the medal-winning performances, performances that are honored, the person ends up feeling like he faked it. Like he basically hood-winked everybody else.   (Miller 2000)

The emotions whirl, panic rises, a red mist descends, the green-eyed monster takes over and we are no longer free agents. There must be many people who feel they faked it when they receive undue credit for acting under the influence of a mere gut reaction. Perhaps Kuldeep Singh does too.

Worse still, for those who want to preserve free will, we need to understand that emotional responses are not entirely an internal affair. This helplessness is reinforced by the ethical climates in which we breathe. Envy is the basis of democracy, says Russell, and as Rozin observed, "Disgust becomes, in many ways, the emotion of civiliza-tion, in the sense that much of the civilizing process involves devel-oping distinctions between animals and humans". He goes on "it's hard to imagine civilization and culture without disgust, the sense of what's inappropriate" (Penn SAS 1997). Internal becomes external and these *external* dark forces and ethical climates that guide our preferences and behaviour can be alarmingly influential.

External "dark forces"

... "And who is my neighbor?" Jesus replied, "A man was going down from Jerusalem to Jericho, and he fell among robbers, who stripped him and beat him and departed, leaving him half dead. Now by chance a priest was going down that road, and when he saw him he passed by on the other side. So like-wise a Levite, when he came to the place and saw him, passed by on the other side. But a Samaritan [a religious outcast], as he journeyed, came to where he was, and when he saw him, he had compassion. He went to him and bound up his wounds, pouring on oil and wine. Then he set him on his own animal and brought him to an inn, and took care of him. And the next day he took out two denarii and gave them to the innkeeper, saying, 'Take care of him, and whatever more you spend, I will repay you when I come back.' Which of these three, do you think, proved to be a neighbor to the man who fell among the robbers?" He said, "The one who showed him mercy." And Jesus said to him, "You go, and do likewise."

(Luke 10:29–37)

What *makes* people go and do likewise, or not? In a classic study Daniel Batson and John Darley told a group of students at Princeton Theological Seminary that they were each to give a talk that would be recorded in another building. On the way to the recording room, each young seminarian encountered a "victim" slumped and coughing in a doorway, and apparently in desperate need of help. What the students didn't know was that they were secretly being divided into groups. Some of them were told they were late and should hurry; some were told they had just enough time to get to the recording room; and some were told they would arrive early. The experiment had a piquant twist in that half of the subjects were assigned to talk on the Good Samaritan parable, while the others were assigned a different topic. They were also categorized according to their religious outlook. The results were striking. The only thing that made a difference to the seminarians' willingness to help was time. Nearly two-thirds of the subjects who had time stopped to help, less than half of those in a slight hurry stopped, and only a tenth of those in a great hurry stopped. It made no difference whether or not the students were talking about the Good Samaritan; nor did it matter what their religious outlook was.

We need to remind ourselves that the "good" are often just those who are lucky enough to have time on their hands. But we don't. We commit the fundamental attribution error, where traits loom much larger than context, as discussed in Chapter 1. The secret pressures of context are much more prevalent than we tend to assume because we stare at the figure and ignore the ground. Yet as with other illusions, it takes a great deal of reminding to think our way past them.

> The librarian carried the old woman's groceries across the street. The receptionist stepped in front of the old man in line. The plumber slipped an extra $50 into his wife's purse. Although you are not asked to make any inferences about any of these characters, chances are that you inferred that the librarian is helpful, the receptionist rude, and the plumber generous. Perhaps because we do not realise the extent to which behaviour is shaped by situations, we tend to spontaneously infer such traits from behaviour.
>
> (Kunda 1999, quoted in Harman 2003: 3)

Worse still, once the illusion is in place it sticks: we decide that someone is helpful or rude and a "confirmation bias" kicks in discounting contradictory evidence while accepting confirmatory evidence too uncritically. And so while people swim through ethical and cultural contexts that hugely constrain the moral choices they make, they ignore them and zero in on judging individual bad apples and good eggs. Some humility would be in order. The librarian carrying groceries in the example above might look less helpful if he were in a hurry. As the novelist Fay Weldon commented, you can believe you are a nice person before you have children; after you have children you understand how wars start.

The same goes for many other contextual factors. If a member of my group (in-group member) does something negative I will tend to specify it as a one-off case, whereas if someone outside my group (out-group member) does the same I will tend to generalize this to their group. A sexist man is likely to judge bad drivers asymmetrically according to their gender. Only the woman driving badly is "typical"; a man running a red light might be an "idiot" but would not be representative of men in general. The reverse happens with a positive act: done by an out-group member we see it as a particular case, but by an in-group member as a generalizable trait. *Homo credens* can also differentiate between in-group and out-group on the slimmest of criteria (eye colour is plenty). Once these conditions are in place the consequences are potentially immense.

Most notoriously we are alarmingly prone to switching off our moral judgement in the presence of authority. Anyone who volunteered for social psychologist Stanley Milgram's painfully informative experiments on obedience in the late 1940s was definitely in the wrong place at the wrong time. His experiment was framed as a "learning task" and involved the volunteers believing they were administering electric shocks to "learners" (actors in fact) who were hidden from view, behind a wall, but quite audible. Milgram expected that few of his subjects would go beyond administering "Very Strong Shock" (150 volts) despite his authoritative white coat and his firm reminders to "Please continue with the task". But in a typical study all forty subjects went beyond that shock level, despite the learners' cries of pain. Only five stopped at the 300 volt level labelled "Extremely Intense Shock" when the learner started pounding on the wall. Four more stopped at the next stage, 315 volts, after more pounding. Two stopped at 330 volts, when the learner made no response at all. One stopped at 345 volts and another at 360 volts. The twenty-six remaining subjects, two thirds of the total group, continued on to the maximum 450 volts. There was no logical place to stop, so the participants continued and reached a point they would never have countenanced before they walked into Milgram's experiment. As a result of this influential work Milgram reworked Hannah Arendt's famous description of Adolf Eichmann's complicity in the Holocaust in *Eichmann in Jerusalem* into the concept of an "agentic state" in which we suspend our capacity to make informed moral judgements and relinquish responsibility for what we do to whoever is in authority. (It is ironic to use the term "agentic" to describe a lack of agency.) He concluded that "Arendt's conception of the banality of evil comes closer to the truth than one might dare to imagine" (1974: 23).

Mark Twain once observed that when people are at liberty to choose, they will choose to emulate their peers. Research agrees with his mordant observation: people agree with statements about the length and shapes of lines that they know to be false simply to be in line with the majority. And even if they are not in a hurry they will not intervene to help if they are aware there are others around who might do so (this is known as the bystander effect). We conform, compare, judge, dilute our agency, stand by or intervene with respect to the presence or absence of other people, and our relationship to them. But if no human is an island we can start to feel that the freely acting moral agent is a mythical beast. If the social context is the determinant of moral "choices" there is nothing left to admire or condemn in them.

Alongside external pressures that shape our judgement, we are equally at the mercy of luck. Bernard Williams coined the term "moral luck" to explain how an action can take different moral significance in respect of its outcomes. If you throw a brick over a wall and it just lands on the grass on the other side, the moral event differs profoundly from one where the brick lands on a baby's head, as does the weight of guilt you must carry afterwards. This concept is a useful reminder that our moral careers are in the hands of luck as well as judgement, and are therefore "beyond our control" in yet another sense.

If we go back to Jim's choice we can see how all the factors we have reviewed that constrain judgement could have helped him escape whipping: the panic and fear he felt that led him to jump; the fact that the captain and the rest of the crew had jumped, which offered the temptations of conformity and peer group pressure.

Even moral luck could have saved him from self-recrimination because nobody died in the end. Yet he still took the full weight of his responsibility as we see in his discussions with Marlowe: "'I had jumped – hadn't I?' he asked, dismayed. 'That's what I had to live down. The story didn't matter.' ... 'It was like cheating the dead,' he stammered." When Marlowe replied that there were no dead: "'And that did not matter,' he said, as stubbornly as you please." Jim stubbornly refuses to shrug off the guilt that comes from feeling he could and should have acted differently, despite the many consolations on offer.

Free enough will

Despite these ominous lessons about human frailty, there are true believers in free will, such as Sartre, who famously claimed that we are in fact condemned to be free. Contrary to all that I have been discussing, he shucks off the constraints of human nature and culture: once we are thrown into the world we are free to make choices. His uncompromising stance (the perfect counterpoint to Gray) invites us to take freedom to the limit, making us responsible for all that we feel or do; we are even guilty of the good we do *not* do. For Sartre, neither actions nor omissions to act can be absolved from responsibility. Even if we are rooted in what he calls "facticity", our situation, our history and biology, it is "bad faith" to deny our ability to transcend these chains. For Sartre, even if Jim had a gun to his head he still had a choice about what to do. Even if he was reacting in blind panic, his actions were entirely up to him. But in light of the discussion in this chapter, this uncompromising view seems to go too far. Does Sartre really want to say that Sophie had a meaningful choice for which we should hold her responsible?

On the other hand doesn't Gray's uncompromising denial of freedom also go too far? It is hard to imagine how Gray can deny free will in practice, even if he does so in theory. Why would he rail against our tendency to embrace illusions if, in fact, there is nothing we can do about them? If we are all merely "deluded animals", why write a book to tell us about it? Why do anything to persuade anyone to think differently at all?

Sartre and Gray represent the ends of a spectrum of views on free will, none of which seems to hold up well enough to scrutiny to get a consensus. Philosophers only seem to converge on one thing when it comes to free will; namely, that there has been little progress made in two thousand years of debate on the matter. Hume called the problem of free will "the most contentious question of metaphysics, the most contentious science" ([1748] 1975: 95). Anyone who feels that we can make genuinely free choices, especially ones for which we can be held morally to account, has to confront the problem of determinism.

Determinism is the view that all events are caused by something prior to them. Our scientific worldview requires that there are causal chains linking events together in a lawful pattern, which extends back in time, and necessitates that nothing can happen otherwise than it does. Even for those who believe in an omniscient God it seems equally hard to make sense of meaningful choices being made when all future and past events are available to that all-seeing eye. On a strictly deterministic view, free will can only be an illusion. When we think we are making choices we are as deluded as Wittgenstein's leaf falling in the autumn wind thinking to itself "Now I'll go this way, now I'll go that". Under this view Lord Jim was indeed "pushed" by events beyond his control, which were rooted in a series of causes that go back to before his birth. His history, his biology, conspired to mean that his leap from the *Patna* at that time was inevitable. For him to have acted differently would have required a different set of causal links, twists of biology, accidents of history, that would have led to a different outcome. But that would have been a different Jim from the one who actually jumped. The actual Jim, determined by what he in fact was, could not have done differently.

Some react to this difficulty by denying the truth of determinism so as to rescue freedom. They point to quantum physics as an example of how some events can be indeterminate and therefore unpredictable. But these "libertarians" (nothing to do with the political label) don't gain much from replacing determinism with indeterminism. It seems hard to imagine a meaningful choice that is randomly generated. Free will in the sense we cherish it is neither pre-determined by prior causes nor the result of a random swerve. Yet there doesn't seem to be a good alternative account. The dilemma is this; either our actions are determined, in which case there is nothing we can do about them, or our actions are random, in which case there is nothing we can do about them. One can see how this ancient problem has bedevilled philosophers since antiquity. The "compatibilists" who want both – to accept the truth of determinism while believing that we are free to choose – struggle to explain how determinism doesn't ultimately swallow accountability, even if the determinism in question occurs further back in time, such as having the good fortune to be a self-consciously brave person rather than a narrowly programmed scorpion.

The pessimists make a strong case against free will, as does the psychological research, it seems, so maybe Valmont had a point. And yet our sense of freedom persists. Rather in the spirit of Samuel Johnson kicking a rock to refute Bishop Berkeley's idealism (the belief that the physical world does not truly exist outside our perceptions of it) modern proponents of free will seem to be reduced simply to insisting on its psychological reality. The pessimists may have the logical upper hand, but don't you just *know* you could freely choose to close this book and throw it across the room? And you may yet do so! Can the pessimists, when they come out of the metaphysical ivory tower and go shopping, really deny the genuine choice they have to buy fish for dinner tonight rather than pasta?

So philosophers can't explain how freedom can exist, while being unable to deny that it does. One interesting suggestion, championed by the philosopher Colin McGinn, is that there are some aspects of human thought that we are not *designed* to understand, and therefore never will. We have minds that are shaped to solve some complex *problems* such as speaking or catching a ball, but when it comes to philosophical *mysteries* we don't know where to begin. The conundrum of free will (a mystery not a problem) will never be solved by a human mind, which never evolved to have the right box of analytical tools for the task, any more than we can think in ten dimensions or a dog can do calculus. This is by no means an uncontroversial view; Daniel Dennett, for instance, whose demystifying ambitions are clear to see in the titles of his books *Consciousness Explained* and *Freedom Evolves*, is dismayed by those who have given up on trying to crack these problems.

Moreover if we place the psychological research under closer critical scrutiny we can see ways that context does not demolish agency. As the social psychologists Alexander Haslam and Steve Reicher have argued, far from giving up agency to authority, people committing evil (genocide, for example) do so knowingly and creatively, if only by turning their actions into virtuous ones first. They observe that:

Until recently, psychologists and historians have agreed that ordinary people commit evil when, under the influence of leaders and groups, they become blind to the consequences of their actions. This consensus has become so strong that it is repeated, almost as a mantra, in psychology textbooks and in society at large. However critical scrutiny of both historical and psychological evidence – along with a number of new studies ... – has produced a radically different picture. People do great wrong, not because they are unaware of what they are doing but because they consider it to be right. This is possible because they actively identify with groups whose ideology justifies and condones the oppression and destruction of others. (2008: 19)

Despite the excuses available to him, we should be grateful for Lord Jim's refusal to shirk his feeling of responsibility; his lack of self-exculpation. His stubborn refutation of the pessimists thus! He may have jumped but he then took the full weight of the consequences of his action. Gray and Marlowe are offering him consolation but he does not take it. Despite the understandable opt-out clause, "it wasn't your fault", I want to salute the way Lord Jim yields himself up to the weight of his action. He believes he could and should have acted differently, and so must accept the consequences; there is something brave in his admission of cowardice.

In the same vein, and despite the arguments of the strong determinists, we struggle with an account that denies Kuldeep Singh's or John Diamond's heroism. Richard Dawkins, in a preface to Diamond's posthumously published attack on alternative medicine *Snake Oil*, clearly demonstrates the contradictions that come from respecting Diamond's wishes while paying homage to the man:

John Diamond gave short shrift to those among his many admirers who praised his courage. But there are distinct kinds of courage, and we mustn't confuse them. There's physical fortitude in the face of truly outrageous fortune, the stoical courage to endure pain and indignity while wrestling heroically with a peculiarly nasty form of cancer. Diamond disclaimed this kind of courage for himself (*I think too modestly*, and in any case nobody could deny the equivalent in his wonderful wife). He even used the subtitle *Because Cowards Get Cancer Too* for his moving *and I still think brave* memoir of his own affliction. (Dawkins 2004: 209, emphasis added)

Dawkins can't help praise the very bravery embodied in Diamond's refusal to be called brave. And surely he speaks for us all. What would life be like if we could never hold each other and ourselves to account for our actions? We need to praise our heroes despite their modesty because, if for no other reason, we want to encourage others, and ourselves, to hew to those standards should the test come. We would like to feel there's a chance we might not curl up when trouble comes our way. We want to act like Singh and not like Jim, and so did Jim. And so we should praise Singh. The painful corollary is that we can't do so without blaming Jim. Dial down the blame and you dial down the praise in the same conceptual move. And, more importantly, it is reasonable to imagine that the post-*Patna* Jim could help *create* the braver self he had hoped to be when he first set out on his adventures: the self-image that Singh is entitled to claim in light of his own actions. Faced with a similar test again Jim might be less likely to fail and, if so, has changed himself in a way that a fatalistic view would not have allowed.

We should take the blame, when we act like Jim, *as much as we can bear*, and give ourselves credit if we find ourselves acting like Singh. We are alterable to some degree and so have reason to strive and to feel guilt. Feeling responsible makes it less likely we will do things we regret and more likely we will do things we need to "find the strength" to do. This is one reason why we can never accept a mechanistic account of our actions; while a scorpion can kill, only a human can commit murder.

So if Jim could have acted differently, what might have made the difference? What nagging thought makes it impossible for Jim to say it was beyond his control? It seems to me there is a clue in Conrad's choice of words for Jim's confession:

"I had jumped." He checked himself, averted his gaze …
"It seems" he added.

Averting our gaze

It was dark; Jim was scared; everyone else in the crew had jumped already. As the lights went out so did his resolve. But he might have acted differently had he caught a glimpse of the people he had left to drown; had he, as we say, caught someone's eye. As Conrad comments:

> It may very well be that, had they been seen, they would have had the effect of a mute appeal – that their glimmer lost in the darkness of the cloud would have had the mysterious power of the human glance that can awaken the feelings of remorse and pity. It would have said "I am here – still here"... and what more can the eye of the most forsaken of human beings say?
>
> (1994: 106)

The "mysterious power of the human glance" is the thing that awakens us and for that reason often the thing we look away from. Daniel Batson, a researcher into moral hypocrisy, illustrates the phenomenon nicely. His subjects were given the opportunity to allocate two tasks, one to themselves and one to a recipient they would never meet. One task was more pleasant to do and the other was dull (see his article "Moral Masquerades" for details of this ten-year research programme). In the first instance, as you might expect, subjects regularly favoured themselves, choosing the positive task nearly 90 per cent of the time while assigning the dull task to the unknown recipient. In a more interesting condition they were offered the option of flipping a coin to determine the assignment of tasks. The ones who chose this method did so because they agreed "it was a fairer way to select", yet the surprising result was that even after the coin toss, they favoured themselves just as often. Miraculously the 50/50 probability of a *normal* coin toss turned into a near 90/10 outcome. And even when the coin was labelled (to stop them retrospectively deciding "heads I win, tails you lose") they *still* assigned the positive choice to themselves to the same degree. Batson found the *only* way to make the assessment come out in line with the expected 50/50 coin toss was when the subject was seated in front of a mirror. It took the mysterious power of the human glance, their own, to defeat their moral hypocrisy.

We have selective blindness when it comes to the small moral tensions we must resolve in everyday life. The colour and shade of these deceptions are often too subtle to see. For example, we are adept at ignoring what we are actually doing so as not to infringe our own rules and have to face the consequences. You tell your child that if she does that one more time you'll send her to her room, and somehow you avert your gaze from the fact that she may have done it just once more to avoid having to mete out the punishment. So now you must have ignored the infringement effectively, and buried your suspicion from your conscious awareness, that is, effectively enough to persuade yourself that nothing really happened. Did the person you bumped into when you walked out of the shop mumble "Arsehole" or not? Do you want to raise the stakes by challenging – "What did you say?" – or do you just ignore it, half-knowing you're ignoring it and feeling faintly cowardly? Or do you persuade yourself that you completely misheard it? Our attention is fickle and self-serving, which is why people who "eat like a bird" seem to put on weight, and money disappears despite the strict budget.

These small deceptions have potentially large consequences for our moral choices. Our lack of attention can lead to quiet acts of insensitivity and callousness. Our incuriosity leaves us unable to sense what matters to other people, and in danger of subtle acts of cruelty. It was George Eliot who wrote that we are "all of us born in moral stupidity". Our concerns loom too large and close to attend well enough to others' fates, as we can see in her subtle reproach from *Middlemarch*:

[W]e do not expect people to be deeply moved by what is not unusual. The element of tragedy which lies in the very fact of frequency, has not yet wrought itself into the coarse emotion of mankind; and perhaps our frames could hardly bear much of it. If we had a keen vision and feeling of all ordinary human life, it would be like hearing the grass grow and the squirrel's heart beat, and we should die of that roar that lies on the other side of silence. As it is, the quickest of us walk about well wadded with stupidity.

There are people, like Eliot, who can help us gain a keener vision: helping us to see strangers as capable of feeling pain and summoning up in us the right kind of emotional response and therefore moral sympathy. Richard Rorty calls these rich interpreters of "the other", the purveyors of thick description, "agents of love". These anthropologists, journalists and above all novelists can enlarge our sympathies by revealing the mysterious power of the human glance and thus inviting us to be better Samaritans. We have some choice over how to direct our gaze: whether to catch someone's eye with it, or avert it. Rorty acutely picks out a startlingly illustrative sentence in Nabokov's *Lolita*, describing Humbert Humbert having a haircut in the small town of Kasbeam:

In Kasbeam a very old barber gave me a very mediocre haircut: he babbled of a baseball-playing son of his, and, at every explodent, spat into my neck, and every now and then wiped his glasses on my sheet-wrap, or interrupted his tremulous scissor work to produce new paper clippings, and so inattentive was I that it came as a shock to realize as he pointed to an easeled photograph among the ancient gray lotions, that the mustached young ball player had been dead the last thirty years. (Quoted in Rorty 1989: 162)

Rorty's own curiosity opens up the sentence thus, and puts less careful readers to shame:

> The reader, suddenly revealed to himself as, if not hypocritical, at least cruelly incurious, recognizes his semblable, his brother, in Humbert and Kinbote. Suddenly Lolita does have a "moral in tow." But the moral is not to keep one's hands off little girls but to notice what one is doing, and in particular to notice what people are saying. For it might turn out, it very often does turn out, that people are trying to tell you that they are suffering. Just insofar as one is preoccupied with building up to one's private kind of sexual bliss, like Humbert, or one's private aesthetic bliss, like the reader of *Lolita* who missed that sentence about the barber the first time around, people are likely to suffer still more. (*Ibid.*: 163–4)

Keener vision is a tough prescription. Paying attention, like looking at the "made in" labels on your clothes and imagining the hands working in the dark that made them, is often unsettling. We can't always pay attention as well as Conrad, Nabokov or Eliot. Even the quickest of us walk about "well wadded with stupidity", our eyes shut, our ears deaf to "that roar that lies on the other side of silence". If there is no omniscient God's-eye view, then all we have are unreliable audiences who might just be looking the other way when you want their attention most. We have to carry the weight of this insignificance, this helplessness, too. Auden shows how the banality of our inattention keeps horrors at bay in his poem "Musée des Beaux Arts" (2002), which he wrote after seeing Brueghel's depiction of the fall of Icarus. He describes how the Old Masters understood suffering's "human position"; how it takes place "While someone else is eating or opening a window or just walking dully along"; and that even during a "dreadful martyrdom" the torturer's horse "Scratches its innocent behind on a tree".

Why did I do that?

"Because it's my nature", says the scorpion." "It's the way of the world, quite beyond my control", says Valmont. "Because I chose to, it seems", says Jim. We don't always know why we did that, said that, thought that, while we are often quick to offer justifications and explanations when asked (with little or no awareness of the processes involved). People are not much like scorpions; we have more options. On the contrary, where animals have instinct we have agency, where they have a past and an ecological niche we have a history and a culture. Along with luck we have judgement, will and choice; and more of them than we can sometimes bear to admit. We may be driven by the four Fs as much as other animals, but these sit alongside the equally deep desires for *meaning* and *credibility* that compete with our more typically animal impulses.

We may be creatures of habit, shaped by those "dark forces", but habits change. It may be true that disgust is a universal human emotion that has evolved for good evolutionary reasons, but it is equally true that surgeons learn to find blood and guts fascinating. They want to get stuck in! We are much more responsible for our habits than we like to admit and we can think our way past them before a new habit springs up (as it will inevitably do). So we know that "it's beyond my control" can't be the whole truth and yet, as we repeat it to ourselves, it starts to become the only truth available. Slippery slope arguments suggest that if you do anything twenty-one times it starts to become a habit. How many more repetitions would it have taken Valmont to think his action was truly beyond his control?

Sometimes we need help to pay the right kind of attention. In the spirit of Spinoza, who teaches us to fight fire with fire (only affect can override affect), Rorty says the way you persuade people to sense the suffering of others is not to appeal rationally (as Kant would) to the essential commonality of human essence (especially since a key ingredient of much oppression comes from denying commonalities and turning people into objects); you do it instead by telling sad and sentimental stories about pain and suffering and loss and mothers and brothers. For this reason he believes that the metaphysicians cannot bring about moral or political progress but rather it is the activists, anthropologists and artists who can pull it off by dramatizing suffering.

We may not be straightforwardly enlightened and approaching the truth – as we have seen, we weren't made that way – but we can *choose*, if only by our own lights, and hope to approach our own goals (contradictory though they may be). And we should recognize that we do, *as much as we can bear*.

The optimistic thought is that our Pleistocene ancestors developed the Plasticine-like ability to live a thousand kinds of life. We must believe in the possibilities of change, the elbow room that we need to help retain will, choice and moral responsibility. There are clearly ways, as Conrad, Eliot, and Rorty show, to open our eyes more often, to reduce our dependency on deception and self-deception. If we pay attention and make ourselves big, we will be more in control. But optimism has its limits. Even Eliot is humbled by the task:

> To be a poet is to have a soul so quick to discern that no shade of quality escapes it, and so quick to feel, that discernment is but a hand playing with finely-ordered variety on the chords of emotion – a soul in which knowledge passes instantaneously into feeling, and feeling flashes back as a new organ of knowledge. *One may have that condition by fits only.*
>
> (*Middlemarch*, emphasis added)

While the attempt to break free of self-serving consolations is highly desirable, we achieve this condition "by fits only". It remains to discuss the limits of any attempt to overcome habitual illusions and our deceptive natures. I turn to these themes in the next and last chapter.

5. To thine own self be true?

So far we have seen that the evolutionary legacy of being a social animal has left us with an anxiety about what and who to trust as well as the finely tuned skills both for detecting cheats and for seeming persuasive. More generally *Homo credens* needs reliable beliefs in order to function, even to the point of believing distortions. Our belief-fixing skills are underpinned by wiring that usefully turns the "blooming buzzing confusion" of sense data into meaningful order, the same process leaving us prone to swallowing illusions. Going beyond merely perceptual illusions these distorting tendencies extend somewhat to cognitive and narrative illusions with implications for how we understand and interact with each other.

On the principle that the most persuasive liars have persuaded themselves first we have evolved the capacity for self-deception. This profoundly useful, although by definition elusive, quality enables us to flatter ourselves and each other that we are nicer and more in control than a closer look would suggest. Look closely and one can glimpse the mixed motives, cognitive dissonance, and general need to bury awkward desires from view. Who was it who said, "A thought-murder a day keeps the psychoanalyst at bay"? The nature of desire is such that it cannot be suitable for polite company, and so we tell self-serving stories that make us look prettier than we are.

We may not like to look closely but our audiences often do. As we saw in Chapter 3, these potent witnesses are alert to signs that a poker face is all bluff and will judge us well or ill depending on how skilfully we manage their impressions of us. But with all the skill in the world we cannot control the judgement of others as much as we would like. These unreliable audiences will judge us irrespective of merit or the amount of control we have over our anxious performances. Sometimes they judge what we like to think of as the content of our character, and other times the mere colour of our skin.

The need to be judged well is an overriding preoccupation, for *Homo credens* needs credit and credibility. A good reputation is more than "nice to have": it is an essential part of the successful life of a social animal. And so to preserve good judgement, when the moral stakes are raised, such as after a regrettable action, we duck and dive: "Mistakes were made", we say (but not by me). We make ourselves small and let ourselves off the hook with alarming ease, averting our gaze from the selfish or cruel choices we like to pretend we did not make.

By drawing attention to the deceptions and consolations that pervade our thought and action it seems obvious to ask what we can do to resist these tendencies. Is it possible to follow Polonius's advice to his son Laertes and be true to "thine own self"? In this concluding chapter I shall explore some options that are available for living well with deception. There are four sections. The first looks at the costs of deceptive tendencies and illusory habits that underpin a solid enough self-image. The second explores some of the ways we might try to break free of them and resolve the mismatch between what we say and what we feel. The final two sections invite you to accept the inevitability of deceptions and distortions in human life despite our best efforts to escape them. If it is the case that we shall always fail to break free, then we need to accept a humbler self-image, and learn to live well in its deceptive light.

Habits of a true self

Most of the time *Homo credens* is well equipped to keep uneasy truths at bay. Adam Phillips invokes Darwin to explore this theme:

"Men are called creatures of reason", Darwin wrote in his notebook in 1839; "more appropriately they would be 'creatures of habit." Habit is evidence of adaptation but habits are disabling when they tacitly assume the future will be like the past. Our survival in what is always a changing environment depends on our capacity to change our habits if need be. Habit ... creates an illusion of predictability; it keeps things the same by turning a blind eye to difference ....

Externally and internally, the struggle goes on to turn unruliness into habit, waywardness into familiarity.

(Phillips 1999: 130–31)

We usually look at ourselves and each other as though from a distance, and at a distance consolatory patterns emerge. With vivid colours, straight lines and a dose of common sense we demarcate heroes, cowards, crooks, Germans, family men, extroverts, terrorists, the fairer sex, true professionals, bad seeds, good friends, national treasures, us, them. And we turn this pattern-making skill on to ourselves with equal facility. We cook up what Rorty calls "final vocabularies" to describe ourselves: a devout Christian, a good mother, a football fan, an Aries, a regular guy, something in the city. These habits of mind offer security and the illusion of stability. For us, change is alarming. Tell someone "You've changed" and it sounds like an accusation. We prefer the safer ground of continuity.

One cannot deny the robust value of common-sense stereotypes. Our folk psychology offers a handy, generalizable theory of what people desire and what they believe without which we could never understand human behaviour. We *need* to generalize. Take rush hour. In general people *desire* money, they *believe* jobs provide money, they *believe* they will lose those jobs if they are always late, and, since lots of people all believe and desire these things at roughly the same time, rush hour happens. This kind of rough and ready stereotyping is necessary for interpreting and predicting human behaviour in the aggregate. But we also know that it is a simplification. If we zoom in on the picture more closely we see more and more explanations for individual and group behaviour. We know that there are people in those crowds who are there for different reasons: children going to school and people going shopping. Go closer still and we can see more complex stories emerge, where beliefs and desires are less easily dissected. Zoom in on a face and see that woman on the underground who has forgotten why she goes to work any longer. She turns up dutifully while wishing she were doing something else; inertia and fear may be better explanations of her daily trek. She may be "something in the city" but look even closer, with the perceptive eye of a novelist, and she starts to look and sound like Eva Khatchadourian, daydreaming about something else entirely, such as how:

> for the duration of our marriage I lived with one terror: that if something happened to you it would break me. But there was always an odd shadow, an underfear, if you will, that it would not – that I would swing off blithely that afternoon to play squash.

And a long period on the couch with a skilled analyst will only make the story more complex and unique to that individual. To simplify is always to leave things out, even if there is always space to debate whether the bit left out is just bathwater; the more careful the description, the less generalizable the story. The relationship between simplification and complexity is linked to our interest in the relationship between appearance and reality. A simplified self-image is a convenient fiction that relies for its credibility on the willing suspension of disbelief of all parties to it. Think, for example, of how we close down the unfolding strangeness of our children by reducing them to mere "chips off the old block". This parental collusion, looking for ways to turn "waywardness into familiarity", is relieved to note that a child always "takes after" someone else. And yet the confederacy is always under threat (as it was for Eva) from a closer look, and the inevitability of change.

The concept of change is so threatening because it undermines the basis for reliability. "To thine own self be true", says Polonius "and it must follow, as the night the day, thou canst not then be false to any man". This dream of a consistent self to which we must be true underpins much of our faith (religious or secular) in honesty, sincerity, authenticity, integrity. Evidence of change, mutability, instability creates unsettlingly fluid images and is often associated with hypocrisy, spinelessness and general untrustworthiness. Yet the fact that we change is so glaringly obvious that we need to shut our eyes tight not to notice. There is nothing final about the vocabularies needed to describe our shifty natures. While we dream up stable enduring traits, we are in fact disturbingly fickle. As discussed in previous chapters, we change profoundly as circumstances alter and as conflicting motives dictate. Our beliefs, desires, skills, reputations and temperaments vary far more than accepted discourse allows. On occasion the generous person will be selfish and greedy, the honest worker will fiddle expenses, the progressive person will be racist, the loyal friend will be bored or embarrassed to have you around, resent your success and hate your partner. Devoted parents will dislike their children, pillars of the community will have fantasies about being sexually assaulted. These common but unmentionable shifts of character are shaped by dark forces we have explored in previous chapters, and must be wished away to preserve reputations and face. Even when we accept the threatening fact of change we shore up the defences that hope to defeat its challenges. Marriage vows promise eternal love that will last; for richer for poorer, in sickness and in health. Yet these promises inevitably understate the significance of the situations that are necessary to keeping them, just as Winston Smith, in George Orwell's *1984*, never thought he would betray his lover with the words "Do it to Julia" until confronted by his phobia of rats.

The sour discomfort we feel in contemplating these awkward truths is a reminder that paying attention can be risky business. A reliable future to believe in is what helps people delay gratification and choose less rashly. But this teleological story, working towards something worthwhile, is threatened when we acknowledge the truth of John Maynard Keynes's remark, "*In the long run* we are all dead". So, to get by, we usually bury our deaths, even though the only thing we can say with certainty about the future is that we shall each die one day, as will everybody we love. In his autobiography, *Experience*, Martin Amis comments on this most enduring of deceptions: "Only in adolescence do we hear the first rumours of our own extinction, these rumours remaining vague until the irrefutable confirmation of the mid-life, when it becomes a full-time job looking the other way". But the murder of his cousin Lucy Partington (by the mass murderers Fred and Rosemary West) jolts his attention and forces him to look. On the day of her funeral:

> I was as glued to the present as Captain MacWhirr in Conrad's "Typhoon", watching the shoes he has flung off "scurrying from end to end of the cabin, gambolling playfully over each other like puppies", as the dark storm begins to show its might. It goes on "He threw himself into the attitude of a lunging fencer, to reach after his oilskin coat; and afterwards he staggered all over the confined space while he jerked himself into it." That lunge. Conrad was the kind of writer who kept his eyes open when most of us would prefer to keep them shut.

As Amis admires Conrad's ability to pay attention he is reminding us how rare this is. We can only do it in fits, and often triggered by those occasional life swerves that take us out of our normality. Habits and convictions are as comforting and robust as they are deceptive. They also depend on a conspiracy of silence in our friends, family and colleagues if they are to anchor us in the stream of shifting colours and shapes in which we swim. And for these anchors to hold they need to feel real. So we must (and are designed to) conceal from ourselves and each other the sheer skill and energy required to keep them in place.

Deception disables us with the occasional feeling of insincerity and bad faith, eroding the grounds for trust, leaving us to live in a cartoon version of the world, seemingly safer and more predictable, but with little understanding and less intimacy. Our consolation prizes bring moral difficulties too. The cost of ducking blame, putting choices "beyond my control", is to become unworthy of praise. And to spend too long with gaze averted is to remain "well wadded with stupidity", and insensitive to the suffering we might be causing. So our useful deceptions are costly. They leave us clinging to a reassuring past but ill equipped to deal with the unpredictable future, estranged from our desires and so less able to meet them or manage them. By averting one's gaze from the aging process, covering up with anti-wrinkle cream, plastic surgery and polite conversation, we become less equipped to handle the challenges of waning powers and sexual desirability. By ignoring how friends change they quietly become strangers to each other with nothing to talk about except antique memories. The awkward truth is that we travel further through our culture and future than we can easily acknowledge; we change far more than we realize and intimations of this makes us fearful. Our status and stasis anxiety encourages us to cling to the small achievements we have rather than break them down and start afresh. We want good reputations, and to feel that the world is more predictable and controllable than it is. The habits work well until they don't work any longer. For Lord Jim in Chapter 4 and for Eva in Chapter 2 we can see how painful circumstances can jolt and even shatter a convenient self-image.

This brittleness is the price we pay for security. An overly well-anchored self-image is too crudely and rigidly drawn, while much of who we are, a patchwork of concealed and contradictory motives, is better evoked with subtler colours and more flexible lines. Our wry smiles and nervous laughs, our daydreams and nostalgia, poignant sympathy and regrets, fugitive anxieties, mixed feelings, shyness and the originality of our children all invite us to notice the half-thoughts, the nuances and the ambiguities of human existence. We usually don't have time or energy to look very closely and carefully. And even when we are tempted, we quickly avert our gaze; for our uneasiness grows as the anchor loses its grip.

Of course there are rhetorical counterpoints that put change at the centre. Management gurus and politicians urge us to embrace change and to be adaptable. To be too rooted in habits, they say, is to be exposed to market jolts in the future, to which the past is not much of a guide. Economist Joseph Schumpeter's recognition that "creative destruction" is the key to economic progress is heralded by many an advocate of the "smashing eggs to make omelettes" school. Creatures of habit need to adjust to ensure economic success as markets and jobs move around. But Darwin, Freud and many novelists go further by taking creative destruction into the psychological realm. They want us to accept the profoundest of changes, leaving no turn unstoned (in the words of theatre critic Kenneth Tynan). These prescriptions move us into the discomfort zone where wishing doesn't make it so, and the truth doesn't care about our egos.

It is true we are not always suckers for a self-serving story. If we are groping around in the darkness of Plato's cave we can at least aim to find a way out into the sunlight. We have mechanisms to think our way past our distorted accounts of ourselves and the world. The philosopher Charles Taylor invokes our capacity for second-order desires to mark us off from the scorpions. That is to say, we make judgements about our judgements rather than merely falling prey to them. For example, I might feel offended by someone while simultaneously recognizing that I have no right to be. Another philosopher, Anthony O'Hear, points out that: "The very fact of being self-conscious about our beliefs, of being in the full sense believers, initiates a process in which we search for what is true because it is true, rather than because it serves some interest of ours" (1997: 30).

But this philosophical prescription is a tough one. The processes of truth-searching range from the truly Popperian scientist scrupulously hunting out evidence that would falsify an elegant theory to more informal ones, such as admitting our failings and overriding self-serving stereotypes. But they run against our grain and are all the more necessary for our frequent failures to adhere to them (while believing we have succeeded). Recent thinkers such as Rorty and many in the continental tradition want us to go further in dropping bad habits, seeing no limit to the unweaving of self-serving beliefs. Even searching for some redemptive idea of the Truth is a suspect habit of mind that we can well do without. These optimists feel that the only thing worth saying about human nature is that we have the capacity to transcend it: that there are no habits so ingrained they cannot be shrugged off. We can alter our destinies through the unfolding conversation of humankind; nothing need be fixed as we find more and more novel ways to cope. The history of ideas as told by such optimists describes a series of "decentrings", where illusions that have underpinned an overblown human self-concept have been replaced by humbler and more useful pictures. In this progressive story Copernicus literally decentred our place in the universe, relegating the earth to a mere planet revolving around the sun. Darwin reconnected us to other animals, while Freud put our egos in their place.

The thought is that all we need do is carry on the process of deconstruction without limit. One suggestion is that we look at ourselves as though visiting an ancient city, as Freud did in *Civilization and Its Discontents*, where he compares Rome to the human mind with a similarly "long and copious past": "an entity ... in which nothing that has once come into existence will have passed away and all the earlier phases of development continue to exist alongside the latest one" (2005: 44). This suggestively helpful metaphor reminds us of the complex blending of old and new that shape human consciousness. To look at Rome is to see both something fixed, and something in transition that looked no less fixed at any other point in its history. Much of who we are is buried, tacit knowledge but leaves its potent traces. Freud is inviting us to be anthropologists in our own culture, and archaeologists of the mind digging up the artefacts that show us where we have come from. The promise of successful excavation is a better understanding of how those Darwinian habits were formed so as to be more able to dislodge or replace them, thus clearing a way to seeing ourselves as work in progress or unfinished business. Rather than being lodged in final vocabularies we get a chance to be more open to the future.

How far can one go in shrugging off deceptive habits? What are the limits, in practice, to self-knowledge and to what we can do to make ourselves anew? In the next section I look at one way we might try to walk the crooked path to sincerity. That is by tackling the problem described in Chapter 2: the awkward fact of desire. The theme of deception, and self-deception, lies archetypally in how we manage, deny, avoid and redescribe our desires. So can we come to terms with our waywardness and resist the bad habit of turning it into familiarity? If we can find a way to shrug off those habitual and distorting ways of seeing there is much to gain, and three things in particular: first, a richer, more interesting and supple (if more unsettling) picture of ourselves; second, a larger sense of moral responsibility for the choices we have made (but we habitually deny) while giving blind chance its due; and thirdly, more hope for change in the future. If the person stuck in a dead-end job, bad relationship or a guilty habit faces up to the choices she has made that might have led to this outcome, rather than ignoring or even accepting them fatalistically, she will be better placed to do something about them by choosing again.

The literary theorist Lionel Trilling defined sincerity simply enough as the "congruence between avowal and actual feeling", but as we have seen this is easier said than done. What we actually feel and what we are prepared to avow, even to ourselves, do not line up well, because it is hard to want what we ought to want. But is it impossible? Or can we work to close this gap, so that there need be nothing to hide?

Managing the unmanageable

In Greek legend the Sirens sang a song so ravishingly beautiful that sailors who passed by their coast would follow their lure until they wrecked their ships on the surrounding rocks and perished. When Odysseus, king of Thebes, heard from Circe the Witch of this delicious danger, he had to experience the Sirens' song for himself. But he heeded Circe's warning enough to ensure he didn't destroy his ship and crew. So he filled his sailors' ears with wax and lashed himself to the mast. As they approached the coast of the Sirens Odysseus was predictably maddened by the alluring music and begged his men to release him, and to sail the ship towards them, to no avail. The sailors couldn't hear the song or his orders, and so they sailed safely by. This near cautionary tail sheds light on the first mechanism of self-control we can use against our perilous appetite for adventure: self-binding.

Odysseus had the clear-eyed foresight to pre-commit his future weaker self while safely distant from the temptation. Had he believed, based on previous triumphs of self-control, that he was strong enough he would have been ill prepared for the challenge. His strength paradoxically came from admitting his weakness, because to ignore your desires is to leave yourself vulnerable to them when opportunity suddenly comes your way. It is a strange fact of human desire that if you have a secret wish you can often find a way to fulfil it by *denying* it; don't think "I'm going to have an affair", just let him touch your hand. In Odysseus's need not to succumb to temptation he had to *admit* its potency. What he understood was that sometimes we need to confess to weaknesses in order to conquer them: in these cases a structural solution is the only answer.

So in that self-binding spirit we find a way to place temptation out of reach as a way to protect our current, well intentioned selves from our future, more weak-willed alter egos: put the alarm clock on the other side of the room so you can't snooze your way through the school run; give the wallet to your spouse on a shopping day; or tell your friends very publicly you have given up smoking so you can't easily light up in their presence. If we burn our boats (like the explorers Hernando Cortes and Tariq Ibn Ziyad, who after landing in Mexico and Gibraltar, respectively, literally did so to keep their men from retreating) we are left with no choice but to plough on.

The political versions of self-binding are the checks and balances that try to keep democratic societies from falling prey to knee-jerk reactions, or self-serving distortions that place short term above long term, us above them. The framers of the US Constitution had a good working knowledge of the frailties of human psychology when they ensured future governments would work within enduring parameters: the separation of church from state and legislature from judiciary, the protection of a potentially awkward free press and a right to free speech were all forms of self-binding. Any society that wants to avoid future corrupting weaknesses would do well to follow this example, while the strenuous efforts of successive administrations to weaken these constitutional binds is evidence enough of their utility in circumscribing absolute power.

Yet on a psychological level, the self-binding of Odysseus can feel like cheating. It doesn't really pass Trilling's sincerity test. Rather than bringing actual feeling into line with avowal, it just controls behaviour. Sincerity demands we have more control over our desires than that, and that we shouldn't have to lash ourselves to a mast to avoid temptation. In any case, this external mechanism is unreliable; arranging the world so we can duck our wishes is too predictable and inflexible and can allow lapses "just this once"; the smoker who is now too ashamed to light up with friends finds herself going out for long walks more often than she used to. We would rather bring the power of self-binding within our own grasp, to make it an act of willpower. Maybe for the strongest addictions we can concede the need for external help (handcuffs, or at least a drying-out clinic), but in general we want to be more in control of our desires than that.

So we attempt a second mechanism of self-control: the personal rule. Instead of putting the alarm clock across the room we compel ourselves to get up as an act of willpower, as a test of character, and do the right thing "even if it hurts". What is at stake here is self-trust and credibility: our ability to make promises to ourselves and others that we can keep even if confronted by the tempting invitation to break them. Hear the Sirens and control yourself. We shoo away temptation and repeat to ourselves that "crime doesn't pay" or that "the devil makes work for idle hands"; the golfer Colin Montgomery (who lost four stone in weight) repeats to himself the personal mantra that "nothing, nothing in the world tastes as good as slim feels" in order to stay svelte.

But this form of *internal* self-binding has its limits too. It might represent a sincere effort to suppress the gap between what we say and do and what we feel, but it doesn't alter the underlying feeling. Do we need to remind ourselves that "crime doesn't pay" to avoid stealing things? Surely we should be intrinsically on the side of the angels and lovers of the good. It is not enough to suppress discreditable feelings; the trick is to transform them. We ultimately want to want what is good for us in the first place, so resisting temptation need not come into play. We want to be proud of our preferences:

to go beyond self-control and to reshape our tastes into a nobler pattern. We *hope* to want what we *ought* to want and thereby hope to gain another thing we deeply want: a good reputation.

This is the third level of self-control to which we can aspire: true character in the Aristotelian tradition that is now described as virtue ethics. With good character we have avowable (that is respectable) desires that we actually feel. To be sure, those things we want to help our reputations are contextualized in different groups; some would prefer to prefer a good novel over *Celebrity Big Brother*, others prefer to prefer kindness over good looks. But whatever the context, to genuinely prefer finer things over tawdry ones is to achieve Trilling's sincerity. We hope to want what we ought to do and so we train ourselves to reshape our tastes. Remember how if you do something twenty-one times it becomes a habit? Bad habits we hope can be supplanted with good ones. We revise our tastes and eventually hope to come to like what is good for us. The child who loved sweets becomes the adult who genuinely loves spinach (and not just because he repeats to himself that "nothing tastes as good as slim feels").

So far so good. But before we get too confident, we need to give desire its lawless due. If desire were so manageable our shelves would not be groaning under the weight of tomes from gurus offering the latest magic path to happiness. The fact we often need tactics like those used by Odysseus and Montgomery should remind us that there are limits to shaping tastes and the reputations we might like to deserve. Desire is nothing if not hard to control:

> I can will knowledge, but not wisdom; going to bed, but not sleeping; eating, but not hunger; meekness, but not humility; scrupulosity, but not virtue; self-assertion or bravado, but not courage; … commiseration, but not sympathy; congratulations, but not admiration; religiosity, but not faith; reading, but not understanding.   (Farber 2000: 79)

These attempts at "willing what cannot be willed" give a clue into how intrinsically hard it is to get what you want. The philosopher John Elster in his book *Sour Grapes* articulates this slipperiness very nicely with the example of insomnia:

> First, one tries to will an empty mind, to blot out all preoccupying thoughts. The attempt, of course, is self-contradictory and doomed to fail, since it requires a concentration of mind that is incompatible with the absence of concentration one is trying to bring about. Secondly, upon understanding that this is not going to work, one tries to induce a state of pseudo-resignation to insomnia. One acts, that is, as if one were persuaded that sleep is going to elude one, by taking up a book, having a snack or a drink, etc. But at the back of one's mind there is always the idea that one can cheat insomnia by ignoring it, and that the cheerful indifference to sleep will make sleep come at last. But then, thirdly, one understands that this is not going to work either. Next, real resignation sets in, based on a real, not a sham, conviction that the night will be long and bleak. And then, finally and mercifully, sleep comes. For veteran insomniacs, who know the game inside out, the last stage never comes. They know too well the benefits of resignation to be able to achieve it.   (1983: 45)

It seems there is something oxymoronic about the idea of "getting what we want", let alone wanting what we ought to want. Managing desire is self-contradictory because desires are rooted in emotion, and emotions cannot be entirely voluntary. As we saw in Chapter 1 they evolved for a purpose: to solve commitment problems by being hard to manipulate. So trying to will what cannot be willed creates anxiety as in the case of Sartre's over-attentive pupil, who tried too hard to look like a good student by looking up and nodding, taking assiduous notes, keeping his ears wide open and "so exhausts himself in playing the attentive role that he ends up no longer hearing anything". Worse still sometimes these efforts at self-control can create the opposite effect of the one we are searching for; trying to look dignified can make you look ridiculous, and trying not to laugh can give you a hernia. Sometimes work does not, and should not, work. Going back to *Kevin*, Eva discovered this heartbreaking disappointment in the most cherished, valorized and "natural" of all relationships: that between mother and child. As she explains to her husband:

> I know you doubt me on this but I did try very hard to form a passionate attachment to my son. But I had never experienced my feeling for you, for example, as an exercise that I was obliged to rehearse like scales on the piano. The harder I tried the more I became aware that my very effort was an abomination.

Controlling the uncontrollable is such a problem that many have gone to great lengths to abolish desire in the first place. Think of the hair shirt traditions of self-denial so common in the world's religions, ranging from self-flagellation to the medieval monk Origen cutting off his own genitals: just keep a lid on it for now and be rewarded in the next life. The attempt to eradicate desire, and to govern oneself minutely by rules, is doomed because an overly successful mechanism for control, one that obliterates that desire, will be self-defeating. To have too much control is to undermine our capacity for pleasure by burying impulsiveness under compulsiveness, which when cemented into workaholism or procrastination or miserliness, can close us down for years. However painful the pursuit of our desires can be, there is a general reason that makes it worse to suppress them too thoroughly. This is because belief, logic and reason have no point unless attached to desires and goals. Unless we are capable of yielding to our desires rather than controlling them we will lose our plot, with no reason to get out of bed in the morning, and nothing to hope for. As Hume insisted, reason should and always will be slave to the passions. Our intelligence only has a point if it is shaped by what we want; and what we want is not entirely up to, or adequately understood by, us.

Without wanting, without goals, daring to hope and enthusiasms, life starts to look lifeless. With this in mind we have conjured up a consolatory myth called "contentment" that promises desire without waywardness. Contentment offers the promise of being able to want what you have, but as we saw in Chapter 2 the meaning of want implies lack. Why, after all, does familiarity breed contempt? Long-lasting contentment is a reassuring myth, but it is inherently unstable and short-lived and easily overturned by listlessness, or the pain of unexpected social comparison with its stabs of jealousy. Our pleasures, in fact, become less valuable to the extent that we can bring them under our control, since that very control will ultimately undermine the appetite itself. To keep desire alive *requires* that we limit how much control we try to have over it. The problem with wanting it quick and easy, or here and now, is that when it is all too easy or quick the pleasure fades. Think of how much pleasure comes from anticipation or from gambles that pay off. Reward depends on doubt and delay. If you won every time you took a risk, it would no longer be pleasurably risky; if you knew that you would always win a game in advance you would lose interest and try something else. As Phillips has it, "the rich have to find their poverty". The psychiatrist George Ainslie generalizes the point:

> [A] too-powerful will tends to undermine its own motivational basis, creating a growing incentive to find evasions. The awkwardness of getting reward in a well-off society is that the creation of appetite often requires undoing the work of satisfying appetite. (2000)

And so, if we cannot defeat our desires, nor live without them, nor reliably shape them into a more civilized form, it seems that deception and self-deception are necessary for keeping discontents at bay. Avowals and actual feelings will never fully meet, and we shall never be truly sincere.

Necessary illusions

The fact that we can see Rome as a "psychical entity" helps us to imagine being effective mental archaeologists. Wittgenstein makes a point about language rather like the one that Freud makes about the mind:

> [A]sk yourself whether our language is complete; – whether it was so before the symbolism of chemistry and the nota-tion of the infinitesimal calculus were incorporated into it, for these are, so to speak, the suburbs of our language. (And how many houses or streets does it take before a town begins to be a town?) Our language can be seen as an ancient city: a maze of little streets and squares, or old and new houses, and of houses with additions from various periods: and this surrounded by a multitude of new boroughs with straight rectangular streets and uniform houses.   (1953: §18)

To recognize that our mind and language is like an ancient city will remind us that they are furnished with habits that have been created at different times in our history and that they change constantly despite seeming continuous. It invites us to believe we can over time shrug off deceptive bad habits and live with muta-bility. But to diagnose the need for excavation is not the same as doing it, or even knowing how to. The crookedness of human consciousness means that a direct approach is seldom effective.

As Wittgenstein also observed: "In the actual use of expressions we make detours, we go by side roads. We see the straight highway before us, but of course we cannot use it, because it is permanently closed" (*ibid.*: §426).

As we have seen in the example of desire the "straight highway" to sincerity is permanently closed. The more general problem with the grander ambition to shrug off our illusions is that it sits ill with the unselfconscious beliefs and goal-directed action of healthy human life. We have populations of believers and doubters in our minds (good angels and bad, as well as naive, impulsive and wiser counsellors) and they jostle for our attention. The believers are easily undermined by the doubters; destroyed by them often. But once belief is destroyed by the acid of cynicism we are left (like Eva, Kevin and Lord Jim) with nothing. We are nothing without belief, so we rove around for things worth believing in: friends, children, undying love, being true to ourselves, contentment, getting it right. Without the myths of continuity, stability, reliability and true selves we become uneasy, self-conscious and unhappy. Uniforms, job titles, rituals, clichés and stereotypes, along with status (and stasis) symbols of all kinds, offer tools for adhering one way or another to a final vocabulary that won't slip from our grasp. Even if ambitions to overturn these illusions are logically possible they are psychologically grandiloquent. The serious attempt to live without illusion, to drop our "deceptive and compulsive sanities", is disorientating and induces a nauseating vertigo. Too much self-knowledge and realism are not healthy for good living.

In his recent novel *Any Human Heart*, William Boyd has given a rare and sustained view of a life largely unadorned by consolatory storytelling. He uses the device of a journal to tell the (fictional) life of Logan Mountstuart, a minor literary figure, which spans most of the twentieth century. "We keep a journal", says Logan, "to entrap the collection of selves that forms us, the individual human being". With this device, entrapping (not explaining or unifying) a collection of selves, Boyd creates a sense of time as it is experienced forwards, unlike most retrospective accounts (fictional or otherwise) with their beginnings, middles, ends, and one thing leading to another. A "true journal", Logan says:

> doesn't record an ideal progression but a more riotous and disorganised reality in which various selves jostle for prominence. Isn't this how life turns out, more often than not? It refuses to conform to ... the narrative needs that you feel are essential to give rough shape to your time on this earth.

In the book the future arrives unannounced and undescribed. It only takes on "rough shape" after the fact, and barely even then. The plot is barely a plot and is full of loose ends that don't get tied down. Friends literally come and go, like opportunities. It is full of uncontrollable luck and with very little moral in tow. True love is vanishingly rare and when it comes can't be protected from vanishing again. The haunting thing about Logan is how he makes depressingly real the theoretical idea that we are work in progress, unfinished, evolving. His language ages, from pretentious schoolboy to middle-aged cynic to serene sage (three of the many selves he becomes). The people and preferences appearing and disappearing from his life and memory, and his reactions, which subtly change over time, show just what it is like to believe the Rortyan idea that a self is not solid, but a "centreless web of beliefs". Reading *Any Human Heart* is to discover that the language of integrity, reliability and certainty now feels like a comfort blanket we've invented for ourselves. As our categories melt, so do our plots. So does our sense of direction. We start to sound like Logan for whom it was all too optional, as he wanders aimlessly, vaguely baffled by events and the smallness of a life, and numbed by mute emotion and alcohol.

Novelists and poets can show us how to rip off the covers that give rough shape to our lives, and allow the world's nonsense to pierce us with strange relation, as the poet Wallace Stevens advised. They show us the literally unbelievable truth that Logan's life is just like our lives, even if it is not possible or desirable to think of it like that. In a letter to his brothers Keats called this "Negative Capability": "that is when man is capable of being in uncertainties, Mysteries, doubts without any irritable reaching after fact and reason". But even the poets and novelists who can, in fits, break down old habits are usually locked into consolatory beliefs of their own. They need something else to hang their projects on to, something to aim at, such as integrity, originality and authenticity, that banishes what literary critic Harold Bloom called their "anxiety of influence". One might argue that one of the things about being "merely human" is the desire to reach beyond ourselves, even if the possibility of doing so is illusory. So if Nietzsche was right to say that "convictions are more dangerous enemies of truth than lies", those same convictions, especially the rose-tinted ones of a looking-glass self, are what we need to keep the show on the road.

Shiftiness and shadiness don't seem like good language to use about a self because *Homo credens* needs psychological belief crutches. While Sartre may argue that we should have the courage to live out the consequences of an atheists' life, it is Dennett who better describes us as having a "sweet tooth" for God. I would expand this to include a sweet tooth for God substitutes, such as fate, tradition, progress, posterity, the simple truth and the real me, which create the right kind of certainty. Without such consolations there is nothing to admire, no purpose worth pursuing and no one to love. The placebo effect of our bouyant "believings in" keeps *Homo credens* afloat. Our authenticity, such as it is, depends not as Rorty has it on self-creation, but paradoxically on losing ourselves unselfconsciously in our illusory patterns. Who wants to be a realist if only the depressed have that level of insight and self-knowledge? So we tell tall tales that show us as nicer and more in control than we are, that populate the commonsensical world with goodies, baddies, us, them and other chips off various blocks. Without robust enough illusions a self has no validity. For the lucky majority the looking-glass self is a rose tinted one.

The problem is that without robust illusions we can't function, and yet detecting their illusory qualities makes them less robust. The various techniques we use to keep the truth at bay, to keep our reputations flying high, require that we don't see the machinery. In his book *Freedom Evolves* Dennett describes the scene in the film *Dumbo* where the young elephant with big ears discovers he can fly by flapping those ears but only after one of the crows gives him a "magic" feather to hold in his trunk. Dumbo's feather is necessary for him to take the leap of faith. Dennett imagines one of the crows whispering to Dumbo that the feather isn't really magic, and spoiling everything, and the audience looking on shouting out as one "Stop that crow!":

> In the eyes of some, I am that crow. Look out, they warn. This person is up to some serious mischief, however well intentioned. He insists on talking about topics that are better left unexplored. "Shhh! You'll break the spell." This admonition is not just for fairy tales; it is sometimes quite appropriate for real life. A fact-laden disquisition on the biomechanics of sexual arousal and erection is not a good topic during foreplay, and reflections on the social utility of ceremony and costume are unwelcome in a funeral oration or wedding toast. There are times when we are wise to divert our attention from scientific detail, when ignorance is indeed bliss.   (2004: 14)

Too much reality can be too much to bear. Of course Dennett, as philosophers will, suggests we can and should let go of that feather. We shouldn't need a childish belief-crutch when a more adult and truer version of events is available. And of course he is right. The philosophical tough prescription is good medicine especially if you want your belief crutches not to be kicked away by someone who has better evidence and a stronger argument.

But even the philosophers will deceive themselves; we all do. Idealization has always been the enemy of understanding our "crooked timber". And Kant, who could diagnose the problem so eloquently and warn philosophers against resembling the light dove, which "cleaving the air in her free flight, and feeling its resistance, might imagine that its flight would be still easier in empty space" (1933: A3 B7), would nevertheless ask us to follow categorical imperatives that require us to be more than human. A less idealized but more robust self-image is one where every self and every relationship into which it enters is inevitably riddled, peppered, flavoured, mired in or sustained by deceptions. The idealized, over-hygienic dreams of unencumbered speech are best left out of the human story. As Wittgenstein puts it: "We have got onto slippery ice where there is no friction and so in a certain sense the conditions are ideal, but also, just because of that, we are unable to walk. We want to walk so we need friction. Back to the rough ground!" (1953: §107).

We always carry feathers, but the feathers we clutch are designed to be invisible to us, so we think we can fly by ourselves. Rather than Dumbo, who could have flown without that feather, we are more like the cartoon character Wiley Coyote, who, sprinting off the edge of a cliff, can keep running on thin air as long as he doesn't look down. Only when there is a breakdown do we see the machinery, and need to look down, and fall.

In the comedy of embarrassment we watch bad technique played out in front of us and can laugh painfully in the dark, relieved that it is not us looking like *The Office*'s David Brent and Steve Coogan's character Alan Partridge, with their awkwardly mixed motives poking out for all to see, but uneasily aware that we don't want our own technique to come under similar scrutiny. We call this genre of comedy "painfully funny" because we see our uglier reflections in the crooked glass: the view normally hidden under tactical smoke and reflected in more flattering mirrors.

Here is an example from *The Office*. Tim and Dawn have a quiet and growing flirtation, which trades on the fact that Tim maintains an ironic distance from the mundane reality of Slough industrial estate. They both believe he is destined for bigger and better things, and she listens admiringly of his grand plans to leave and start a degree in psychology. But things change. Sometimes we compromise. Here he is redescribing those initial ambitions to a doubting but considerate Dawn.

Dawn: So when are you leaving me?

Tim: Erm, probably won't be for quite a while.

–Autumn?

–Probably not.

–I thought you wanted to go back to university and everything?

–Yeah, I will, but there's a slight bit of a change in plan.

–Oh, right.

–David's made me senior sales clerk.

–Wow. I thought you wanted to be a psychologist.

–Oh, yeah, but senior sales clerk, it's £500 guaranteed extra a year, and if I do a bit of networking, then there's every chance I could be in David's chair in 3 years.

–And all that talk about moving on in the world?

–No, I said moving up, yeah, moving up. Moving up can mean within an internal ladder framework, or sideways to external, then up. You know, you gotta look at the whole pie, vis-à-vis my current life situation.

(Gervais & Merchant 2003)

The sweet-natured Dawn doesn't think less of Tim, even though she is surprised. If she had been meaner she could have dismantled that "internal ladder framework" rung by rung. We need better technique than Tim's. Orwellian reinventions of history to keep us looking nice and in control must be skilful and plausible if they are to hold up. One thing needs to lead to another in a more seamless flow if we're going to get other people to look "at the whole pie". With better mechanisms of deception and self-deception we can start to believe in integrity, loyalty, bravery, contentment, noble sentiments and true love. Where our technique fails us the vertigo sets in again and we need a little help from our friends.

Living well with deception

In December 1983 the science (and science fiction) writer Isaac Asimov finally agreed, after worsening angina, to have a triple bypass operation on his heart. He was understandably anxious and, as befits a scientific cast of mind, asked how the surgeon could cut into his aorta and coronary arteries without blood gushing out in a flood.

> Oh no. He said. Hasn't anyone explained? After we expose the heart we stop it.
> I felt myself turn a pretty shade of green. You stop it?
> Yes, we give it a heavy slug of potassium ion, and cool it, and it stops beating…
> How do you start the heart again? What if it won't start?
> That can't happen. He said confidently. The heart wants to do nothing but start. We have to work hard to keep it still. As soon as we let the potassium wash out, it starts right in again
> …   (Asimov 1987: 193–4)

This is a good way to think about our propensity for creating illusions. As our hearts can't stop pumping blood so our minds can't stop pumping illusions. As we've seen in this chapter, the desire to tame our heart's desire is doomed to fail; desire wriggles free every time. The humbling conclusion we should accept is that *Homo credens*'s self-deluding mind bounces back into action as soon as the philosophy washes away.

However hard we work to keep it still, the belief muscle keeps pumping. Remember how perceptual illusions continue despite our second-order knowledge that this is all they are? So we needn't worry too much about vertigo and feeling scattered. It's a little like worrying that we'll never be able to enjoy an optical illusion again now we know how it works.

We are condemned to believe, deceive, make sense by cooking the facts, and to look at the world and each other from our highly defended parapets. Deception and self-deception are intrinsic to self-consciousness and, as Nietzsche recognized, we can only look out at the slit windows of other people's defences while unable to see our own. We will always hide our contradictory thoughts and desires from others, from ourselves, all the while managing impressions of each other in pursuit of a good reputation:

> Self-observation. Man is very well defended against himself, against his own spying and sieges; usually he is able to make out no more of himself than his outer fortifications. The actual stronghold is inaccessible to him, even invisible, unless friends and enemies turn traitor and lead him there by a secret path. (1994: §491)

There is no undeceptive way to live, but there are ways to live with deception without feeling corrupted. Tim was lucky to find that Dawn did not "turn traitor". In all relationships, mutual knowledge is a dangerous thing, which is why we use veiled speech. Fading looks, waning powers, mismatches of expectation, boredom, disappointments and inconsistencies require tact and a complicated kindness. Fidelity not so much to the truth but to each other is what is at stake. By contrast honesty can be a brutal weapon. As Tennessee Williams once commented, "all cruel people describe themselves as paragons of frankness".

This conclusion sounds like an appeal to put solidarity over truth. It is not quite as simple as that for two contrasting reasons. First, unless we use the techniques of truth-seeking to support our self-serving stories (evidence and good arguments make for more persuasive claims than mere assertion), those anchors start to fail and we end up all at sea. Second, we do not have that much choice in the matter; we cannot completely wish those illusions away. To think that we can is merely another (quite helpful) illusion. There is no way to live without deception and self-deception, but there are ways to do so that are less or more malign. *Homo credens* needs to know what motives are in play before judging someone's faithfulness, and thus whether to punish, ignore or collude. A lovely example of this shift in perspective can be seen in two extant versions of Shakespeare's Sonnet 138 ("When My Love Swears that She is Made of Truth"). In his book *1599: A Year in the Life of William Shakespeare*, James Shapiro juxtaposes the two versions to reveal contrasting approaches to deception in relationships. The first version was first published as the opening poem in Shakespeare's poetry anthology *The Passionate Pilgrim*:

When my love swears that she is made of truth,
I do believe her (though I know she lies)
That she might think me some untutored youth,
Unskilful in the world's false forgeries.
Thus vainly thinking that she thinks me young,
Although I know my years be past the best:
I smiling, credit her false speaking tongue,
Outfacing faults in love, with loves ill rest.
But wherefore says my love that she is young?

And wherefore say not I that I am old:
O, love's best habit is a soothing tongue,
And age in love, loves not to have years told.
Therefore I'll lie with love, and love with me,
Since that our faults in love thus smothered be.

In this cynical version the poet echoes Nietzsche's observations about sordidly self-serving tendencies to which we are all quite prone. The speaker is selfish and exploitative. Here we can see the lopsided nihilism of deception, which gives nothing away and focuses single-mindedly on playing the charade more cleverly. But Shakespeare, with the subtlest of edits, turns this sentiment into a more redemptive variant.

When my love swears that she is made of truth
I do believe her, though I know she lies,
That she might think me some untutor'd youth,
Unlearned in the world's false subtleties.
Thus vainly thinking that she thinks me young,
Although she knows my days are past the best,
Simply I credit her false-speaking tongue:
On both sides thus is simple truth suppress'd.
But wherefore says she not she is unjust?
And wherefore say not I that I am old?
O, love's best habit is in seeming trust,
And age in love loves not to have years told:
Therefore I lie with her and she with me,
And in our faults by lies we flattered be.

The previous version is depressing because deception is toxic to the relationship, but in this later one there is something redemptive in the reciprocal knowledge that tongues must be governed. Conspiracies of silence are not necessarily malign. Eva may have observed how much lying in a marriage comes from simply keeping quiet, and the same goes for parents, children, friends, colleagues and more, but that lying can be well or badly intended as we see in the two versions of this sonnet. Shapiro concludes that in the first version of the poem the speaker:

> is only fooling himself when he "lies with love"; in the revised version he lies with his love in both senses of the word, their playful falsehoods securing their affection. In the new ending their love is forgiving not smothering. This sense of mutuality, of merging selves, rings out in the chiming sound of the concluding couplet: "she … me … we … be". (2006: 199)

The second version, the more benign, less corrosive interpretation of deception and self-deception, invokes Goffman's "sweet guilt of conspirators". Dawn and Tim, after all, knew that they couldn't say all that they knew. To be trustworthy does not mean you hold honesty to be the best policy. It means that you are *faithful* to the person who trusts you: aligned with or allowing for their needs and wants. There are loyal lies and honest betrayals, because we all need illusions to feel good about ourselves and to maintain a sense of self-continuity. And no doubt this humbling counsel invites cynics to use the ubiquity of deception in self-serving ways too; conniving to be kind. We lie to others in order to comfort them or to protect their emotional wellbeing, as well as to mislead and exploit.

Our audiences are the judge in each case. If I judge you ill, then, with Nietzsche, I can say that "not that you lied to me, but that I no longer believe you, has shaken me". If I judge you well then I become your co-conspirator and simply credit your false-speaking tongue. But the guilt is sweet, keeping us, as Heaney wrote, "allied and at bay". In this light we can see how the unavoidable fact of our deceptive natures can be used to inform a more subtle, complex but potentially more robust self-image: faithful to our crooked timber, and less dependent on the false promise of a straight story.

Further reading

Deception broadly defined, as I have attempted to explore it in this book, covers a wide terrain that has been well traversed by philosophers, psychologists, psychoanalysts and behavioural economists as well as by novelists and poets. For those looking to start with a crystal clear and entertaining discussion of the deceptive quirks and foibles of human nature Steven Pinker's books *How the Mind Works* (1998) and *The Stuff of Thought* (2007) are hard to beat (even if you don't swallow the whole evolutionary story they tell). Daniel Dennett's books *Consciousness Explained* (1993) and *Freedom Evolves* (2004) engage with similarly demystifying themes with equal wit and brio. Robert Frank's book *Passions within Reason* (1988) is the best account of how the emotions, in particular, serve as guarantors of our sincerity. And David Livingstone Smith's book *Why We Lie* (2004) is a stimulating and entertaining synthesis, ranging from evolutionary psychology to psychotherapy, that begins to capture the sheer range of insights relevant to this theme.

The self-contradictory nature of human desire and the deceptions that result from this are cleverly detailed in Jon Elster's books – especially *Sour Grapes* (1983) and *Ulysses and the Sirens* (1979) – as well as the remarkably insightful *Breakdown of Will* by George Ainslie (2001). William Ian Miller's *Faking It* (2003) is a more personal, although equally scholarly, reflection on the hypocrisies that accompany daily life. It seems to me, though, that the most subtle and insightful reflections on the conflicts of our inner lives come from psychoanalysts. I recommend Leslie Farber's essay "Lying on the Couch" in his book *The Ways of the Will and Other Essays* (2000) and pretty much anything written by Adam Phillips, although *Monogamy* (1996), *Darwin's Worms* (1999) and *Going Sane* (2005) all have particular relevance and appear in the text above. Phillips's fluid and aphoristic style comes closest (*pace* the novelists) to describing the subtle conflicts that pepper human consciousness.

The everyday deceptions that we use to keep our relationships functioning and our reputations flying high depend a great deal on social technique. There is no better chronicler of these daily duplicities than the sociologist Erving Goffman, and his key works are *The Presentation of Self in Everyday Life* (1959) and *Stigma* (1963). Richard Sennett is a more contemporary source and his recent book *Respect in a World of Inequality* (2003) does a magnificent job of detailing the demanding and obscure tasks that shape human interaction.

The topic of deception directs our attention to some of the most intrinsically subtle and complex features of our moral psychology: not least because the self-deception that I describe is by definition hard to spot. The novelists and poets who show this subtlety in action rather than freeze it in analytic aspic are indispensable to understanding the phenomena. Beyond Lionel Shriver's *We Need to Talk About Kevin* (2005), George Eliot's *Middlemarch* (1996) and William Boyd's *Any Human Heart* (2003), I'd recommend Flaubert's *Madame Bovary*. Richard Rorty's discussion of Nabokov on cruelty in *Contingency, Irony and Solidarity* (1989) and Martha Nussbaum's discussion of Dickens and Proust in *Love's Knowledge* (1992) are wonderful examples of how philosophy that attempts a closer look at our crooked timber can be enriched by literature.

References

Ainslie, G. 2001. *Breakdown of Will*. Cambridge: Cambridge University Press.

Amis, M. 2003. *Koba the Dread*. London: Vintage.

Amis, M. 2001. *Experience*. London: Vintage.

Aronson, E. 1980. *The Social Animal*. San Francisco, CA: W. H. Freeman.

Asimov, I. 1987. *The Subatomic Monster*. London: Grafton.

Auden, W. H. 2002. *Selected Poems*. London: Faber.

Batson, D. 2008. "Moral Masquerades: Experimental Exploration of the Nature of Moral Motivation". *Phenomenology and the Cognitive Sciences* **1**: 51–66.

Batson, D. & J. Darley 1973. "From Jerusalem to Jericho: A Study of Situational and Dispositional Variables in Helping Behaviour". *Journal of Personality and Social Psychology* **27**: 100–108.

Benson, O. & J. Stangroom 2006. *Why Truth Matters*. London: Continuum.

Billig, M. 2005. *Laughter and Ridicule: Towards a Social Critique of Humour*. London: Sage.

Blackburn, S. 2005. *Truth: A Guide for the Perplexed*. Harmondsworth: Penguin.

Bloom, H. 1997. *The Anxiety of Influence*. New York: Oxford University Press.

Boyd, W. 2003. *Any Human Heart*. Harmondsworth: Penguin.

Bruner, J. S. 1986. *Actual Minds, Possible Worlds*. Cambridge, MA: Harvard University Press.

Buller, D. 2005. *Adapting Minds: Evolutionary Psychology and the Persistent Quest for Human Nature*. Cambridge, MA: MIT Press.

Cheever, J. 1990. "Journals". *New Yorker* (13 August): 29.

Conrad, J. 1994. *Lord Jim*. Harmondsworth: Penguin.

Cosmides, L. 1989. "The Logic of Social Exchange: Has Natural Selection Shaped how Humans Reason? Studies with the Wason Selection Task". *Cognition* **31**: 187–276.

Davidson, D. 1990. "The Structure and Content of Truth". *Journal of Philosophy* **87**(6) (June): S279–328.

Davidson, D. 2004. *Problems of Rationality*. Oxford: Clarendon Press.

Dawkins, R. 2004. *A Devil's Chaplain*. London: Orion.

Dennett, D. C. 1993. *Consciousness Explained*. Harmondsworth: Penguin.

Dennett, D. C. 2004. *Freedom Evolves*. Harmondsworth: Penguin.

Diamond, J. 1999. *C: Because Cowards Get Cancer Too ...*. London: Vermillion.

Ekman, P., R. J. Davidson & W. V. Friesen 1990. "The Duchenne Smile: Emotional Expression and Brain Physiology II". *Journal of Personality and Social Psychology* **58**: 342–53.

Eliot, G. 1996. *Middlemarch*. Oxford: Oxford University Press.

Elster, J. 1979. *Ulysses and the Sirens: Studies in Rationality and Irrationality*. Cambridge: Cambridge University Press.

Elster, J. 1983. *Sour Grapes: Studies in the Subversion of Rationality*. Cambridge: Cambridge University Press.

Farber, L. H. 2000. *The Ways of the Will and Other Essays*. New York: Basic Books.

Flaubert, G. 2003. *Madame Bovary*. Harmondsworth: Penguin.

Fodor, J. 1983. *The Modularity of Mind*. Cambridge, MA: MIT Press.

Foot, P. 2002. *Moral Dilemmas: And Other Topics in Moral Philosophy*. Oxford: Clarendon Press.

Ford, R. 2006. *The Sportswriter*. London: Bloomsbury.

Ford, R. 2006. *Independence Day*. London: Bloomsbury.

Ford, R. 2007. *The Lay of the Land*. London: Bloomsbury.

Foucault, M. 2001. *Fearless Speech*. Cambridge, MA: MIT Press.

Frank, R. 1988. *Passions within Reason: The Strategic Role of the Emotions*. New York: Norton.

Freud, S. 2005. *Civilization and its Discontents*. New York: Norton.

Gervais, R. & S. Merchant 2003. *The Office: The Scripts Series 2*. London: BBC Books.

Giddings, P. 1997. "Parliament and the Executive". *Parliamentary Affairs* **50**(1): 84–96.

Gilbert, D. 2006. *Stumbling on Happiness*. London: HarperCollins.

Goffman, E. 1959. *The Presentation of Self in Everyday Life*. Harmondsworth: Penguin.

Goffman, E. 1963. *Stigma: Notes on the Management of Spoiled Identity*. Harmondsworth: Penguin.

Gould, S. J. 1991. *Bully for Brontosaurus*. Harmondsworth: Penguin.

Gray, J. 2002. *Straw Dogs: Thoughts on Humans and Others Animals*. London: Granta.

Grice, P. 1989. *Studies in the Way of Words*. Cambridge, MA: Harvard University Press.

Harman, G. 2003. "No Character or Personality". *Business Ethics Quarterly* **13**(1): 87–94.

Haslam, S. A. & S. D. Reicher 2008. "Questioning the Banality of Evil". *The Psychologist* **21**(1): 16–19. www.thepsychologist.org.uk/archive/archive_home. cfm?volumeID=21&editionID=155&ArticleID=1291 (accessed May 2008).

Heaney, S. 1998. "Clearances". In his *Opened Ground: Poems 1966–1996*. London: Faber.

Hume, D. 1975. *Enquiry Concerning Human Understanding*. Oxford: Clarendon Press.

James, W. [1890] 1981. *The Principles of Psychology*. Cambridge, MA: Harvard University Press.

Kant, I. [1781] 1933. *The Critique of Pure Reason*. London: Macmillan.

Kant, I. [1785] 1996 *Groundwork of the Metaphysic of Morals*. In *Practical Philosophy*, M. J. Gregor (trans.). Cambridge: Cambridge University Press.

King, B. 2006. *The Lying Ape: An Honest Guide to the World of Deception*. Cambridge: Icon Books.

Kunda, Z. 1999. *Social Cognition: Making Sense of People*. Cambridge MA: MIT Press.

Larkin, P. 1988. *Collected Poems*, Anthony Thwaite (ed.). London: Faber.

Lemert, C. & A. Branaman 1997. *The Goffman Reader*. Oxford: Blackwell.

Levinas, I. 1998. *Otherwise than Being: Or Beyond Essence*. Pittsburgh, PA: Duquesne University Press.

Loftus, E. 1994. *The Myth of Repressed Memory: False memories and Allegations of Sexual Abuse*. New York: St Martin's Press.

Marar, Z. 2003. *The Happiness Paradox*. London: Reaktion Books.

McGinn, C. 2002. *The Making of a Philosopher*. London: Simon & Schuster.

Milgram, S. 1974. *Obedience to Authority*. New York: Harper & Row.

Miller, L. 2000. "The Mystery of Courage". Interview with W. I. Miller, author of *The Mystery of Courage*. http://archive.salon.com/books/int/2000/10/25/miller/ (accessed April 2008).

Miller, W. I. 2003. *Faking It*. Cambridge: Cambridge University Press.

Milner, M. 1969. *On Not Being Able to Paint*. New York: International Universities Press.

Neimark, J. 1995. "It's Magical. It's Malleable. It's ... Memory". *Psychology Today* (Jan/Feb). http://psychologytoday.com/articles/pto-19950101-000021.html (accessed May 2008).

Nietzsche, F. 1966. *Beyond Good and Evil*, W. Kaufmann (trans.). New York: Vintage.

Nietzsche, F. 1994. *Human, All too Human*. Harmondsworth: Penguin.

Nussbaum, M. C. 1992. *Love's Knowledge: Essays on Philosophy and Literature*. Oxford: Oxford University Press.

O'Hear, A. 1997. *Beyond Evolution: Human Nature and the Limits of Evolutionary Explanation*. Oxford: Oxford University Press.

Pascal, B. 2004. *Pensées*. Whitefish, MT: Kessinger Publishing.

Penn Society of Arts and Sciences. 1997. "Food for Thought: Paul Rozin's Research and Teaching at Penn". *Arts and Sciences* (Fall). www.sas.upenn.edu/sasalum/newsltr/fall97/rozin.html (accessed May 2008).

Phillips, A. 1996. *Monogamy*. London: Faber.

Phillips, A. 1999. *Darwin's Worms*. London: Faber.

Phillips, A. 2000. *Promises, Promises: Essays on Literature and Pscyhoanalysis*. London: Faber.

Phillips, A. 2005. *Going Sane*. Harmondsworth: Penguin.

Pinker, S. 1998. *How the Mind Works*. Harmondsworth: Penguin.

Pinker, S. 2007. *The Stuff of Thought: Language as a Window into Human Nature.* Harmondsworth: Penguin.

Plato. 2005. *Protagoras.* Harmondsworth: Penguin.

Plato. 2007. *Republic.* Harmondsworth: Penguin.

Reicher, S. D. & S. A. Haslam. 2006. "Tyranny Revisited: Groups, Psychological Well Being and the Health of Societies". *The Psychologist* **19**: 146–50.

Rorty, R. 1989. *Contingency, Irony and Solidarity.* Cambridge: Cambridge University Press.

Rothstein, B. 2000. "Trust, Social Dilemmas and Collective Memories". *Journal of Theoretical Politics* **12**: 477–501.

Rozin, P. & A. E. Fallon. 1987. "A Perspective on Disgust". *Psychological Review* **94**: 23–41.

Rozin, P. & C. Nemeroff. 1990. "The Laws of Sympathetic Magic". In *Cultural Psychology*, J. Stigler, R. Shweder & G. Herdt (eds), 205–32. Cambridge: Cambridge University Press.

Runciman, D. 2008. *Political Hypocrisy.* Princeton, NJ: Princeton University Press.

Russell, B. 1940. *An Inquiry into Meaning and Truth.* London: Allen & Unwin.

Sartre, J.-P. 1970. *Nausea.* Harmondsworth: Penguin.

Sennett, R. 2003. *Respect in a World of Inequality.* New York: Norton.

Shapiro, J. 2006. *1599: A Year in the Life of William Shakespeare.* London: Faber.

Shriver, L. 2005. *We Need to talk about Kevin.* London: Serpent's Tail.

Smith, D. L. 2004. *Why We Lie: The Evolutionary Roots of Deception and the Unconscious Mind.* New York: St Martin's Press.

Taylor, C. 1985. *Human Agency and Language.* Cambridge: Cambridge University Press.

Tilley, C. 2006. *Why?* Princeton, NJ: Princeton University Press.

Trilling, L. 1972. *Sincerity and Authenticity.* Cambridge, MA: Harvard University Press.

Tversky, A. & D. Kahneman 1983. "Extensional Versus Intuitive Reasoning: The Conjunction Fallacy in Probability Judgment". *Psychological Review* **90**: 293–315.

Williams, B. 1981. *Moral Luck.* Cambridge: Cambridge University Press.

Wittgenstein, L. 1953. *Philosophical Investigations.* Oxford: Blackwell.

Index